ULTIMATE
BASKETBALL

ULTIMATE BASKETBALL

BY JOHN HAREAS
FOREWORD BY BILL WALTON

DK PUBLISHING, INC.
LONDON, NEW YORK, MUNICH,
MELBOURNE, AND DELHI
Project Editor Anja Schmidt
Senior Art Editor Susan St. Louis
Designer Tai Blanche
Art Director Dirk Kaufman
DTP Coordinator Milos Orlovic
Production Manager Chris Avgherinos
Picture Researcher Chrissy McIntyre
Proofreader John Searcy
Project Director Sharon Lucas
Creative Director Tina Vaughan
Produced for DK Publishing, Inc. by
Senior Art Editor Claire Legemah
Imaging and Photo-manipulation Nick Harris

NBA Publishing   Charles Rosenzweig, Mario Argote, Michael Levine,
David Mintz, Matthew Krautheim
NBA Entertainment Photos   Joe Amati, David Bonilla, Pam Costello,
John Kristofick, Bennett Renda, Brian Choi, Scott Yurdin
NBA Entertainment   Adam Silver, Gregg Winik, Paul Hirschheimer,
Marc Hirschheimer, Rob Sario, Tony Stewart
Photo Editor   Joe Amati
Writer   John Hareas
NBA Entertainment Staff Photographers   Andrew D. Bernstein,
Nathaniel S. Butler, Jesse D. Garrabrant

Published by the Penguin Group
Penguin Group (USA) Inc., 375 Hudson Street, New York, New York 10014, U.S.A.

Penguin Books Ltd, Registered Offices: 80 Strand, London WC2R 0RL, England

First published by DK Publishing in 2004
04 05 06 07 08 10 9 8 7 6 5 4 3 2 1

A catalog record for this book is available from the Library of Congress.
A CIP catalogue record for this book is available from the British Library (UK)

ISBN: 0-7894-9743-3 (Hardcover)
0-7894-9866-9 (Library Binding)
UK ISBN 1 4053 0409 X
Color reproduction by Colourscan, Singapore
Printed by Toppan Printing Co. (Shenzhen) Ltd.

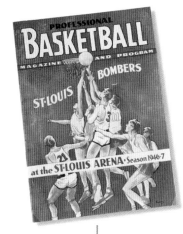

CONTENTS

Basketball—The Ultimate Game

These pages contain all there is to know about the history of basketball—the game I found so many years ago growing up on the edge of my hometown, San Diego, California. My father was a social worker, an adult educator, and a music teacher; my mom was our town's librarian. We didn't have much in terms of material possessions, we had to learn how to create our own fun. I was an extremely shy youngster and was very reluctant to interact with others because of my severe speech impediment. Consequently, I used the game of basketball as a shield. The game became my religion and the gym was my church.

Basketball was perfect for me. I discovered this wonderful world when I was just eight years old, tagging along after my older brother, Bruce. I found in one outlet something that would satisfy all my cravings. The game offered everything, including opportunities for teamwork, hard work, creativity—and for mollifying the desires of my insatiable imagination.

Academics were always very easy for me as both my parents were college graduates who constantly stressed education as the number one focus in our home. But I silently waited for the first chance to get out to the court and chase the universal dream of trying to become the best player in the land. It was there that I discovered the endless reasons why basketball is so perfect in all ways: for the disadvantaged, it requires minimal equipment; for the verbally challenged, it demands no spoken word; for the impatient, you only have to wait for the opening tip; and for those who can never get enough, basketball is truly the one game that is fun to practice—even by yourself. What you need in this game, more than anything else, is an innovative mind.

I learned to live this game from the start—from every backyard court in our neighborhood to all the public schools, parks, and recreation centers throughout San Diego; from playing international ball just across the border in Tijuana to playing as a high-school player on the US National Team in the 1970 World Championship in Yugoslavia; from UCLA and Pauley Pavilion to the NCAA Championships; and finally to the grandest of all stages, the NBA.

This dream stems from the source of all life—the ball. The same ball that we grew up with, dribbling to and from school; lying on your bed shooting the imaginary shots, fantasizing

about playing against the best, beating the best, and eventually becoming the best. And wonderfully, there is nothing that can stop you from achieving your goals, other than your not wanting to put the time and effort in.

Basketball also teaches the great lessons that shape not only our individual lives but civilization as well: discipline, organization, commitment, sacrifice, learning methods, leadership, responsibility, communication, teamwork, respect, dealing with adversity, and delivering a peak performance on command. Like life itself, the game encompasses all the things that you really need to know. But as in life, when you're playing you rarely have any idea of what it is that you're actually learning. It wasn't until much later down the road, when I was forced to deal with life's toughest issues, that I became aware of how important all those lessons really were.

Basketball is so much more than just a game, more than just a jump shot, a rebound,

or a loose ball. Basketball, like life, is the ultimate transition game, in which you never stop running, never stop chasing your dreams, never stop spending all you have trying to figure out how to be first to the ball.

What could be better than racing up and down the court with sweat poring off your body, the steaming heat, the self-generated wind blowing through your hair, back and forth barking at refs, coaches, and teammates alike? Soaring through the air in pursuit of happiness, satisfaction, and possession of the ball. And unlike anything else that I've found in my life, when things aren't going your way, there is nothing more effective than the perfectly placed elbow directly into the midsection of your opponent to get you back into the game.

Basketball has come a long way in the search for and the drive to play the perfect game. From Dr. James Naismith's invention of an activity to provide healthy indoor exercise during the brutal winter months to the earliest days in the game's history, when young players like John Robert Wooden would convince his mom to make from scratch his first basketball, sewn from old rags scavenged from around the family farm in Indiana. Today, basketball spans the globe with players competing at unprecedented levels in the ultimate pleasure palaces of L.A.'s Staples Center, Houston's Toyota Center, San Antonio's SBC Center, Miami's American Airlines Arena, New York's Madison Square Garden, and Boston's FleetCenter. Yet it's still really all the same. It's still ballplayers, with the ball in their hands as an extension of their minds, trying to determine their future. What could be better than the daily participation in the celebration of sport and life where happiness and optimism are the reigning emotions that allow one's dreams to come true?

Through a lifetime lived in the prism of this great game, I have come to realize that there is nothing more rewarding than being part of a special team. The NBA now provides all of us that chance on a constant basis. To witness the broadcasts, to be in the arenas, to be involved in the remarkable feats and accomplishments of the world's greatest athletes playing the world's greatest game is really the story of being part of the planet's biggest pick-up game with everybody working their way up the ladder.

And best of all, at the end of the day, you get the self-satisfaction of collapsing into bed with the biggest smile on your face after leaving everything you have out on the court, knowing that you actually did something today and that you get to wake up tomorrow and do it all over again. Because this is one game that never really ends. Plus, you simply can't even come close to ever reaching the outer limits of available possibilities.

Does anybody want to play?

Bill Walton

Bill Walton (top) and the Portland Trail Blazers swatted the Philadelphia 76ers' attempt at an NBA title in the 1977 NBA Finals.

Timeline: 1891–1958

IN 1891, DR. JAMES NAISMITH invented a game that proved to be an instant success and was played in YMCAs across the country. Seven years later, the National Basketball League (NBL) formed, and though it lasted only five seasons, other leagues soon emerged on the East Coast in the late 1890s and early 1900s. In the 1940s, arena owners looking to fill dates on their calendar formed the Basketball Association of America (BAA). The league eventually became known as the National Basketball Association (NBA), as it absorbed teams from the NBL in the late '40s. The first official BAA game debuted in 1946, sparking a new era in basketball.

December 21, 1891
Eighteen players, 13 rules, two peach baskets, and a 1–0 final score was the result of the first "basket ball" game, created by Dr. James Naismith.

November 1, 1946
The Basketball Association of America, later the NBA, debuted as the New York Knickerbockers visited the Toronto Huskies for the league's inaugural game.

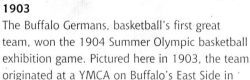

January 7, 1926
Founded by Abe Saperstein (left) in 1926, the Harlem Globetrotters, originally named the Savoy Big Five, became one of basketball's most popular teams.

June 6, 1946
Maurice Podoloff, president of the American Hockey League, was appointed president of the Basketball Association of America. He negotiated a merger of the BAA and NBL to form the NBA in 1949.

1903
The Buffalo Germans, basketball's first great team, won the 1904 Summer Olympic basketball exhibition game. Pictured here in 1903, the team originated at a YMCA on Buffalo's East Side in 1895 and played until 1925.

1891   **1903**   **1926**   **1946**

April 12, 1954
The Minneapolis Lakers ruled the NBA as the league's first dynasty, winning five titles in six years, the last of which was earned on April 12, 1954.

March 2, 1951
The first NBA All-Star Game tipped off in Boston. Walter Brown, the Boston Celtics' owner (center), was instrumental in making the game a reality.

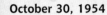

October 30, 1954
The 24-second shot clock debuted during the 1954–55 season, and made an immediate impact. NBA teams increased their scoring by an average of 13.6 points.

April 13, 1957
The greatest dynasty in NBA history was officially born when the Boston Celtics won the first of 11 NBA championships in 13 years. The Celtics' incredible run included eight titles in a row.

1951   **1954**   **1957**

Timeline: 1959-1970

THE GREATEST BASKETBALL dynasty in NBA history was in full bloom by the 1960s. The Boston Celtics picked up where they left off, as they steamrolled to eight consecutive titles. In 1967, the Philadelphia 76ers took the championship—the only gap in Boston's otherwise perfect decade of nine titles out of ten. While the Celtics undeniably staked their claim as the greatest team of its era, the decade also showcased NBA greats who weren't named Bob Cousy, Bill Russell, John Havlicek, Bill Sharman, or K. C. Jones. The dominance and all-around brilliance of such future Hall of Famers as Wilt Chamberlain, Oscar Robertson, Jerry West, and Elgin Baylor emerged in the '60s, as well as great rivalries. The Lakers and Celtics met six times in the NBA Finals, while the Chamberlain–Russell match-up was the ultimate showcase in offensive and defensive skills.

March 2, 1962
Wilt Chamberlain shocked the basketball world (and the New York Knicks) when he scored 100 points in a single game. The 1961–62 campaign also showcased the brilliance of Oscar Robertson of the Cincinnati Royals, who averaged a triple double—30.8 points, 12.5 rebounds, and 11.4 assists—for the entire season.

September 1, 1963
J. Walter Kennedy was named NBA President and eventually saw his job title change to Commissioner in 1967. Under Kennedy, the NBA expanded coast to coast, swelling from 9 to 18 teams.

April 9, 1959
The greatest championship run in all of professional sports officially began on this date. The Boston Celtics won the 1959 title on their way to an unprecedented eight championships in a row.

1959   1960   1961   **1962**   **1963**

February 17, 1968
The Naismith Memorial Basketball Hall of Fame officially opened its doors to the public in Springfield, MA, the birthplace of basketball. The Hall of Fame already boasted a class of 66 individuals and four teams since it had first welcomed members in 1959, nine years before the building opened.

April 28, 1966
The Boston Celtics saw their incredible streak of NBA championships grow to eight after the 1965–66 squad defeated the Los Angeles Lakers in seven games during the 1966 NBA Finals. The Celtics' reign briefly came to an end the next season as the Philadelphia 76ers defeated them in the East Finals.

May 5, 1969
The NBA's ultimate winner, Bill Russell (left), retired as a player after leading the Boston Celtics to the franchise's 11th NBA title in 13 seasons. Russell served as a player-coach for Boston's last two championships. No player in NBA history has matched Russell's 11 titles.

1966   **1968**   **1969**

Timeline: 1970–1989

THE 1970s USHERED IN A NEW era of basketball—no one team dominated its competition like the Boston Celtics had in the '60s. Instead, the '70s became known as the Decade of Parity, as teams took turns hoisting the NBA championship on a yearly basis. The 1970s also saw the American Basketball Association come to an official close following the 1975–76 season, as four of its teams joined the NBA. The arrival of two rookies named Larry Bird and Magic Johnson prior to the 1979–80 season lifted the NBA to new heights of popularity as the Celtics and Lakers dominated the competition, winning eight out of the possible 10 championships in the '80s. While the Bird–Johnson rivalry was heating up the league, a new crop of players named Jordan, Olajuwon, Barkley, Malone, Ewing, and Robinson were putting their stamp on the game as well.

June 17, 1976
The American Basketball Association, featuring its trademark red, white, and blue ball, ceased operation after nine seasons. Four teams—the Denver Nuggets, Indiana Pacers, New York Nets, and San Antonio Spurs—joined the NBA prior to the 1976–77 season.

May 7, 1972
The Los Angeles Lakers officially closed the book on one of the greatest seasons in NBA history after defeating the New York Knicks in five games in the 1972 NBA Finals. The Lakers won an unprecedented 69 regular-season games, which included an NBA record of 33 in a row.

April 30, 1975
Larry O'Brien was named the third commissioner of the NBA. He oversaw the absorption of four American Basketball Association teams in 1976, and, along with David Stern as point man, was instrumental in developing the historic collective bargaining agreement with the NBA Players Association.

1979–80 Season
The NBA welcomed two high-profile rookies named Larry Bird and Magic Johnson, who joined the Boston Celtics and Los Angeles Lakers, respectively. The Lakers won the NBA title that season. The league also introduced the three-point field goal.

June 30, 1985
In order to accommodate the growing number of visitors each year, the Naismith Memorial Basketball Hall of Fame moved from the campus of Springfield College into a larger facility nearby.

April 8, 1989
An International Basketball Federation (FIBA) vote opened competition to NBA players so they could play in international events, such as the Olympics and the World Championship of Basketball.

February 4, 1984
David J. Stern became the fourth commissioner of the NBA. Under his leadership, the league has grown from 23 to 30 teams, international interest has blossomed due to NBA players' participation in the Olympics and league initiatives, and NBA games are now televised in 212 countries in 42 languages. Stern also oversaw the launch of the WNBA, NBDL, and NBA TV.

FIBA
We Are Basketball

THE NBA DR

December 13, 1983
The Pistons and Nuggets totaled 370 points in a triple-overtime thriller, which Detroit won, 186–184. This set a record for the highest score by a winning and losing team.

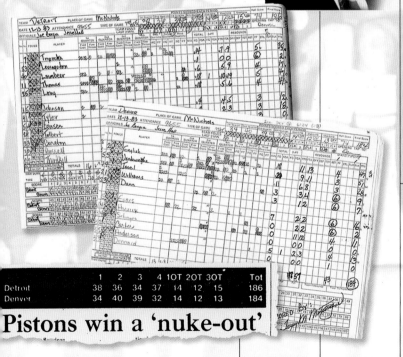

	1	2	3	4	1OT	2OT	3OT	Tot
Detroit	38	36	34	37	14	12	15	186
Denver	34	40	39	32	14	12	13	184

Pistons win a 'nuke-out'

May 12, 1985
The NBA introduced a draft lottery for all teams that failed to qualify for the playoffs. The New York Knicks, which posted a 24-58 record at the end of the 1984–85 season, won the top pick and the rights to select Patrick Ewing of Georgetown.

1983   1984   1985   1989

Timeline: 1990–2003

THE 1990s WAS A DECADE of global growth for the NBA, as players quickly became household names overseas. In 1990, the Utah Jazz and Phoenix Suns tipped off the inaugural NBA Japan Games, marking the first time a major US sports league played a regular-season game outside of North America. The 1992 Barcelona Olympics marked the first time NBA players participated in these historic games, and the US team won by an average of 32 points per game. While the NBA was enjoying new levels of popularity overseas, the Chicago Bulls were making NBA history. Michael Jordan emerged as the best player in the game, leading the Bulls to six NBA championships in eight years, while collecting an array of individual awards. By the time the 21st century rolled around, a record number of international players were testing their skills as members of NBA teams.

April 21, 1996
The Chicago Bulls defeated the Washington Bullets to earn their 72nd victory of the season, establishing a new regular-season record of 72-10.

April 24, 1996
The Women's National Basketball Association was born. The first game between the New York Liberty and the Los Angeles Sparks tipped off on June 21, 1997.

February 1, 1995
John Stockton, the 16th overall pick of the 1984 NBA Draft, surpassed Magic Johnson as the NBA's all-time assists leader, as the Utah Jazz defeated the Denver Nuggets, 129–88.

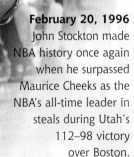

February 20, 1996
John Stockton made NBA history once again when he surpassed Maurice Cheeks as the NBA's all-time leader in steals during Utah's 112–98 victory over Boston.

November 2, 1990
History was made as the Phoenix Suns and Utah Jazz tipped off the Japan Games to open the 1990–91 regular season. The NBA became the first major US sports league to play regular-season games outside North America.

January 6, 1995
Lenny Wilkens surpassed Red Auerbach as the NBA's all-time winningest coach when the Hawks beat the Bullets to give him his historic 939th victory.

1990

1995

199

February 9, 1997
The 50 Greatest Players in NBA History were honored in Cleveland, the site of 1997's NBA All-Star Game.

June 26, 2002
The Houston Rockets select Yao Ming with the first overall pick of the 2002 NBA Draft. The 7-5 Chinese center became the first player from an international basketball league to be chosen as No. 1.

October 28, 2003
The opening-day rosters for the 2003–04 season featured a record 73 international players, from 34 countries and territories, on 26 of the 29 NBA team rosters.

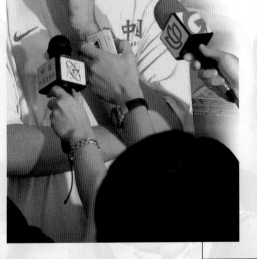

September 2002
The new, state-of-the-art, interactive Naismith Memorial Basketball Hall of Fame opened its doors.

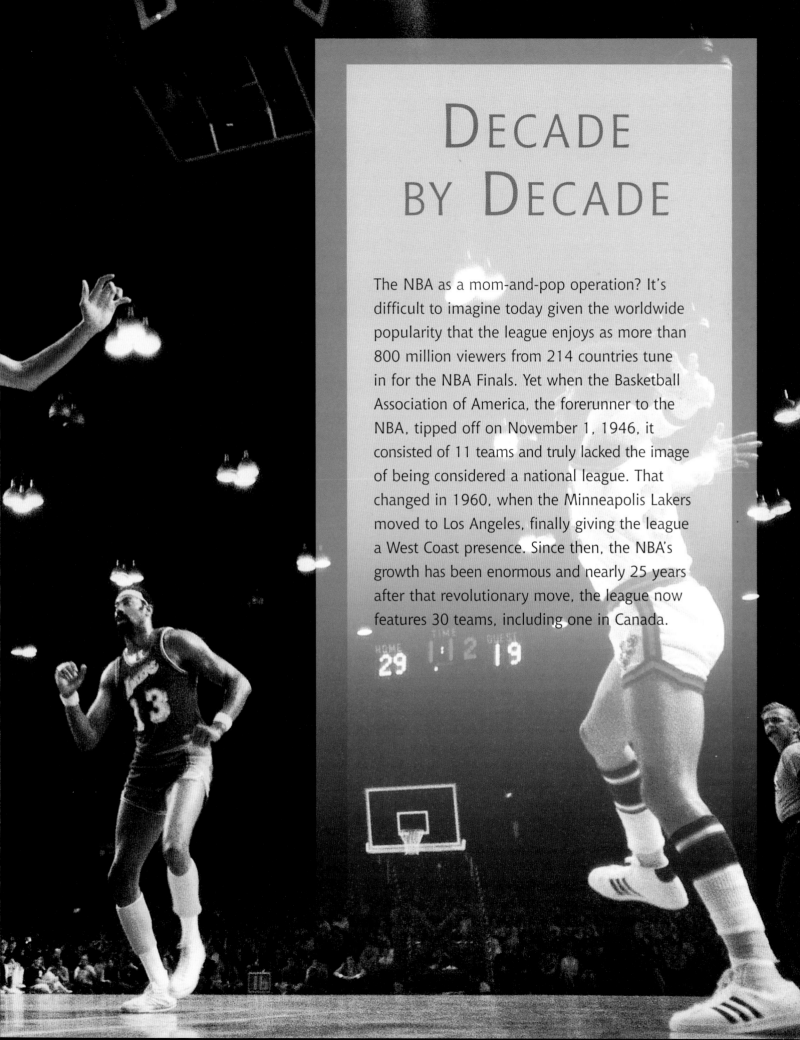

DECADE BY DECADE

The NBA as a mom-and-pop operation? It's difficult to imagine today given the worldwide popularity that the league enjoys as more than 800 million viewers from 214 countries tune in for the NBA Finals. Yet when the Basketball Association of America, the forerunner to the NBA, tipped off on November 1, 1946, it consisted of 11 teams and truly lacked the image of being considered a national league. That changed in 1960, when the Minneapolis Lakers moved to Los Angeles, finally giving the league a West Coast presence. Since then, the NBA's growth has been enormous and nearly 25 years after that revolutionary move, the league now features 30 teams, including one in Canada.

1891–1920

WHO COULD HAVE IMAGINED that an assignment given to Dr. James Naismith in 1891 would become one of the world's most popular games more than 100 years later? The sport's self-effacing inventor was far from a one-dimensional person. This one-time lumberjack, Presbyterian minister, volunteer for the Kansas National Guard, and chaplain in a border war against Pancho Villa, saw the game he created grow rapidly in popularity as the turn of the century approached. Soon, professional leagues and teams emerged, including the Buffalo Germans and the Original Celtics, who dominated the competition. Early professional basketball was marked by a physical style of play, taking place within the notoriously brutal confines of the Cage.

The 13 original rules above were the blueprint of the game Dr. James Naismith invented.

DR. JAMES NAISMITH

In 1891, Dr. Luther Gulick, the head of Physical Education at the School for Christian Workers at the YMCA International Training School in Springfield, Massachusetts, issued a challenge to Dr. James Naismith, one of the school's instructors: come up with an indoor game that would occupy some unruly students during the winter.

Naismith had exactly 14 days to fulfill his supervisor's request. Drawing inspiration from other games such as baseball, football, lacrosse, rugby, and soccer—and his favorite childhood game, "duck-on-a-rock"—Naismith had the pieces in place for "basket ball."

OPENING TIP

How did Dr. James Naimsith go about actually staging the first basketball game in 1891? He had assistance from the school's janitor and secretary, both of whom played a crucial role in the game's development.

Pop Stebbins, the janitor, was responsible for nailing peach baskets to the lower rail of the balcony (10 feet high) on opposite ends of the gymnasium at the International YMCA Training School in Springfield, Massachusetts, while Ms. Lyons, the school secretary, typed up the 13 original rules for Dr. Naismith to use while overseeing the game.

Then the students arrived. They were a lively group of young men who were suffering from more than just a mild case of cabin fever due to the harsh New England winter.

"There were 18 in the class," said Naismith, reflecting on the historic game. "I selected two captains and had them choose sides. I placed the men on the floor. There were three forwards, three centers, and three backs on each team. I chose two of the center men to jump, then threw the ball between them. It was the start of the first basketball game and the finish of trouble with that class."

The game had two 15-minute halves with a five-minute rest in between. In a half an hour's time, only one basket was made.

Eighteen students participated in the first-ever basketball game at the YMCA gymnasium in Springfield. Although the final score was only 1-0, the game was an immediate success.

THE BUFFALO GERMANS

The Buffalo Germans began with six boys who played basketball together at a YMCA on Buffalo's East Side in 1895. They eventually formed one of the most dominant basketball teams in history.

The Germans barnstormed their way to greatness by capturing the Pan American championship in 1901 and an Olympic title in St. Louis three years later. Featuring star player Al Heerdt, Buffalo once won an amazing 111 consecutive games from 1908–1911, including a 134-0 victory over Hobart College.

Their dominance came to an end when the team disbanded in 1929, after compiling a staggering 792-86 record.

They came, they saw, they conquered. The Buffalo Germans are one of only five teams that have been inducted into the Basketball Hall of Fame.

The Cage was not for the meek. Early professional basketball combined a physical style of play on the court with unruly fans off of it.

THE CAGERS

The first basketball cage was made from chicken wire; later versions incorporated steel mesh and metal. Regardless of the material, the end result was often the same: physical, bruising, no-holds-barred basketball. Welcome to the early 1900s, known as the Cage Era, when it was absolutely necessary to wear knee, elbow, and shin pads. Whether they were being knocked cold by no-nonsense opponents, or jabbed by hat pins and burned by cigarettes from overzealous fans, players during this era were tough.

"Players would be thrown against the wire," said Barney Sedran, one of the game's best, "and most of us would get cut. The court was covered in blood."

Later, the introduction of the rope-mesh cage was embraced by players who welcomed a few less nicks and bruises.

THE ORIGINAL CELTICS

One of the most influential teams in basketball history, and one of the best barnstorming teams, the Original Celtics brought national attention to the game of professional basketball and their impact was felt both on and off the court. The team consisted of superior showmen, led by passing whiz Nat

The Original Celtics dominated the competition, winning a national title and barnstorming their way to a 204-11 record during the 1922–23 season.

Holman, and introduced pivot play and switching man-to-man defense to the game. Off the court, the Celtics were the first team to sign players to individual contracts, which prohibited them from jumping teams.

Originally known as the New York Celtics, the team formed in 1914 on Manhattan's West Side and stormed to a 65-4 record during their first year. After disbanding briefly during World War I, they regrouped in 1918 under their new name.

1922–1945

THE 1920s ROARED in with new teams taking center stage. The most prominent were the Renaissance Five and the Harlem Globetrotters, two African-American juggernauts that barnstormed their way to great success on the road, since neither were welcomed into any of the upstart leagues. The American Basketball League featured great teams such as the Clevelend Rosenblums, while the National Basketball League featured great players like George Mikan and one of the game's most visionary owners, Fort Wayne's Fred Zollner.

THE CLEVELAND ROSENBLUMS

The Cleveland Rosenblums were the premier team in the American Basketball League, which was progressive in signing players to contracts, making backboards mandatory, and eliminating the wire cage around the court. The Rosenblums won the ABL's inaugural title in 1925, and were led by John "Honey" Russell, who went on to play in more than 3,200 games during his professional career.

Cleveland received a boost three years later when their rival, the Original Celtics, disbanded and key members switched teams. Joe Lapchick, Dutch Dehnert, and Pete Barry donned the Rosenblum uniform and helped lead Cleveland to their second title in five years. Their dominance continued until the league shut down following the 1931 season.

The Cleveland Rosenblums won three ABL titles in six years and featured greats such as Dutch Dehnert (fourth from left) and Joe Lapchick (fifth from left).

THE HARLEM GLOBETROTTERS

Abe Saperstein had a vision: assemble a team of African-American players and market them by barnstorming the country. Saperstein took ownership of the Savoy Big Five of Chicago, changed their name to the Harlem Globetrotters, and on January 27, 1926, sent them to their first game in Hinckley, Illinois. The team then proceeded to travel the country, racking up victories at every stop.

In 1927, the Trotters compiled a 101-6 record and, to ensure repeat visits, the players entertained the fans by spinning the ball on their fingers, bouncing it off their heads into the basket, or drop-kicking it through the hoop.

The "Clown Princes of Basketball" were also one heck of a basketball team, winning the Chicago Herald World Professional Basketball Tournament in 1939, after defeating the Rens in the semifinal round.

THE RENAISSANCE FIVE

The Renaissance Five were a barnstorming force. From 1923 to 1949, the Rens compiled a 2,588-529 record and once won 88 consecutive games. Founded by Robert J. Douglas, the Rens featured the likes of Charles "Tarzan" Cooper, "Wee" Willie Smith, and Clarence "Fat" Jenkins. They were the first salaried African-American professional team and also the first to win a world title when they defeated the Osh Kosh All-Stars in the World Pro Tournament in Chicago. "To this day, I have never seen a team play better team basketball," said Hall of Famer John Wooden, who played against them when he was a member of the Indianapolis Kautskys.

The NBL featured top players but not top venues, as evidenced by this photo featuring a rather quaint setting at this Detroit Eagles-Sheyboygan Redskins game.

THE NATIONAL BASKETBALL LEAGUE

One of basketball's most successful leagues, the NBL was ahead of its time when it came to corporate sponsorship, featuring such team names as the Akron Firestone Non-Skids, the Akron Goodyear Wingfoots, the Toledo Jim White Chevrolets, and the Chicago Studebakers. The Jim White Chevrolets and the Studebakers featured African-American players on their rosters, and members of the Chicago team also found employment during the week working at the Studebaker plant.

The NBL, which was founded in 1935 under the name of the Midwest Basketball Conference, lasted until the 1948–49 season, when its top teams and players were absorbed by the Basketball Association of America.

FRED ZOLLNER

Fred Zollner, owner of the NBL's Zollner Pistons, was dubbed "Mr. Pro Basketball" by the NBA in 1975, and for good reason. In addition to advocating important rule changes and becoming the first owner to acquire a bench coach or private airplane for his team, Zollner also played a crucial role in the survival of the fledgling NBA in the late '40s and early '50s, contributing financial support, transportation, and personnel during the early years of the league.

GEORGE MIKAN

One of college basketball's biggest stars, leading DePaul University to the NIT Championship and picking up College Player of the Year honors twice during his four-year career, George Mikan was the franchise before the nickname ever came into existence. The 6-10 center signed with the Chicago Gears upon graduating DePaul and picked up where he left off in college—dominating.

Mikan averaged 16.5 points in the National Basketball League, the predecessor to the NBA, and led the Gears to the NBL championship. The Joliet, Illinois, native played only one season in Chicago, as he was assigned to the Minneapolis Lakers, also of the NBL, after the Gears' owner's attempt to create his own league failed.

Mikan continued to ascend as the professional game's first superstar player, leading the Lakers to five titles in six seasons.

George Mikan made a favorable impression during his pro debut with the Chicago Gears, leading them to the NBL championship in his rookie season.

1946: The BAA Is Born

THE 1920s HAD SEEN A WAVE of new arenas built across the US. Operated by hockey owners, these venues provided the backdrop for a new professional basketball league to bloom in the mid-1940s. The movers and shakers of the Basketball Association of America (BAA)—founded June 6, 1946—were men experienced in sports and business who eventually used their expertise to oversee the absorption of six NBL teams and the changing of the BAA's name to the National Basketball Association (NBA). Although this upstart had a long way to go before the arenas would be filled, the foundation of its future success was in place.

WALTER BROWN

After the end of World War II, hockey owners and arena operators decided that professional basketball was the best alternative to fill open dates on their calendars. The success of college doubleheaders gave a strong indication that a professional league, filled with former college stars, would have a real shot of succeeding.

Walter Brown, the president of hockey's Boston Bruins, took the lead in helping form a new professional basketball league, the Basketball Association of America (BAA). Brown was no newcomer to sports management and marketing, having played a major role in the creation of the Stanley Cup and the Ice Capades, and the saving of the Boston Marathon.

Brown served as owner and team president of one of the charter franchises, the Boston Celtics, who played their home games in the Boston Garden, which was also home to the Bruins. Brown played a major role in selecting the team name—as he explained, "Boston is full of Irishmen."

EDDIE GOTTLIEB

Eddie Gottlieb was owner and coach of one of the most successful barnstorming teams of the early 20th Century. The Philadelphia SPHAs (South Philadelphia Hebrew Association) won 11 championships, dominating the Eastern and American Leagues from the late 1920s to the early '40s. Gottlieb then established the BAA, and coached the Philadelphia Warriors to the first league championship. He became the team owner in 1955, and later served as one of the NBA's primary consultants and schedule makers.

MADISON SQUARE GARDEN

One of the greatest assets of the BAA was its collection of arenas, such as New York's Madison Square Garden, located at 49th Street and Eighth Avenue. The third version of the Garden, which was built in just 249 days at a cost of $5.6 million dollars, opened on November 24, 1925. The 18,000-seat arena was the official home of the New York Knickerbockers, who joined the BAA in its inaugural season (1946–47).

Ironically, the Knicks didn't enjoy much home-court advantage in that season, playing only six home games in the "Mecca of Basketball," which was also home to many other events, such as circuses, hockey games, rodeos, bicycle races, and college basketball matches. The Knicks ended up playing 24 of the season's home games at their alternate home: the 69th Regiment Armory.

Bob Davies (right) routinely kept his opponents off balance with his unorthodox moves, and enjoyed a Hall of Fame career.

The Knicks played their first game at Madison Square Garden on November 11, 1946, and lost to the Chicago Stags in overtime, 78-68.

BOB DAVIES

Bob Davies, the 6-1 point guard nicknamed "The Harrisburg Houdini," is often overshadowed among basketball's great playmakers. He was a two-time All-America at Seton Hall before joining the NBL's Rochester Royals in 1945. Davies mesmerized opponents and thrilled fans with his creative ballhandling and passing techniques, whether they were behind the back, through the legs, or over the head. Considered one of professional basketball's greatest showmen, he led the Royals to NBL titles in 1946 and '47—earning MVP honors the second time—and an NBA title in 1951.

MORE GLOBETROTTER FUN

After winning the World Professional Basketball Tournament in 1939, the Trotters really hit their stride in the 1940s, traveling all over the globe, becoming perhaps the greatest basketball draw in the world. This was not lost on the NBA owners promoting the upstart league in the late '40s, who saw an opportunity to bring more fans to the arenas. Team owners often scheduled doubleheaders in which the NBA teams would play in the opener while the Trotters followed as the main attraction.

In the early '50s, the Trotters embarked on their first-ever South American tour. More than 50,000 fans watched the Trotters play at Rio de Janeiro's Estadio Municipal on April 25, 1951. Four months later, 75,000 fans jammed into Berlin's Olympic Stadium to see the Trotters, and were treated to a halftime appearance by Jesse Owens, who was flown in by helicopter to the site where he'd been snubbed by Adolph Hitler in the 1936 Olympics.

Reece "Goose" Tatum signed with the Trotters in the 1940s, and was an instant hit with fans as he became one of the game's ultimate showmen.

RED AUERBACH

Arnold "Red" Auerbach's career path to coaching greatness didn't begin in Boston, but in Washington, DC. The Brooklyn, New York, native coached the Washington Capitols for three seasons in the BAA, winning two Eastern Division titles and compiling a 115-53 record before moving on to the Tri-Cities Blackhawks, where he stayed for one season.

In 1950, Celtics owner Walter Brown hired Auerbach, who shaped the greatest dynasty in NBA history, coaching Boston to nine titles in a 16-year period, while accumulating the most wins in NBA history (938).

1946–1949

ELEVEN FRANCHISES PLAYED in the inaugural 1946–1947 season of the Basketball Association of America (BAA), featuring teams in such markets as Boston, Chicago, New York, St. Louis, and Toronto. The league's first champions, the Philadelphia Warriors, also featured the league's first star, Joe Fulks. During this era, the BAA's chief rival was the National Basketball League (NBL), which didn't have the luxury of showcasing its teams in large arenas such as Madison Square Garden, but did feature top players such as George Mikan of the Minneapolis Lakers. In 1948, the Lakers joined the BAA, which changed its name to the NBA the following year.

Fulks' 63 Points Set BAA Record

By FRED BYROD

Continued From First Sports Page

mock seriousness, to substitute one of his own players for Joe.

Five different Jets — Carlisle Towery, Price Brookfield, John Mandic, Leo Mogus and Jack Eskridge—had tried unsuccessfully to shackle the Warriors' ace. Each fouled him at least once. Joe made nine of his 14 free throws.

JOE HOT AT START

Joe was the hottest at the outset, connecting on six of his first nine tries from the floor. But he never failed twice in a row until late in the second quarter, when he missed on four in a row. Then he racked up No. 13 with a running one-hander.

The Jets had tied the score four times in the early minutes and trailed by only 49-38 at half time, but wilted in the second half before the Fulks deluge.

Late in the third quarter, Joe connected with three successive shots. Shortly afterward, he got another on a tap-in of George Senesky's foul-line miss, and then he passed the Mikan mark of 48 by grabbing a rebound and dropping a jumping one-hander with 1.50 to go in the period.

TWO QUICK GOALS

Obviously dead tired—he hasn't fully recovered from a stomach ailment which has troubled him for the last 10 days—Fulks got up to 59 points with four minutes left. Then he sank his last two baskets in quick succession on a layup, following a pass from Chink Crossin, and a jumping two-hander.

Senesky, who tallied 11 points, was the only other Warrior to break into double figures. Mogus led the Jets with 14.

Just before the BAA's deadline on signing new players, the Warriors added another last night in six-foot-five Jacob Bornheimer, New Brunswick, N. J., resident who played briefly at Muhlenberg College and since then with Utica in the New York State League.

The Sphas defeated the Brooklyn

Long before the institution of the 24-second shot clock, Joe Fulks set a single-game record with 63 points.

FIRST BAA GAME SET TO TIP OFF

Finding an audience for basketball was tough, especially given hockey's overwhelming popularity in Canada, so it was no surprise that the Toronto Huskies tried hard to lure fans to the first-ever BAA game. Tickets ranged from 75 cents to $2.50, and if any fan was taller than Toronto's 6-8 George Nostrand, he or she was granted free admission. The posters worked, as more than 7,000 fans watched the New York Knickerbockers defeat the Toronto Huskies 68–66 on November 1, 1946.

The First Scoring Sensation

Joe Fulks had quite a rookie season. Not only did the 6-5 forward/center lead the BAA in scoring (23.2), he also led his team, the Philadelphia Warriors, to the inaugural BAA championship title as well. Nicknamed "Jumpin' Joe," Fulks was one of the first players to use the two-handed jump shot before switching to a one-handed delivery. Fulks followed up his rookie campaign by winning his second consecutive scoring title (22.1) in 1947–48. In his eight professional seasons, Fulks averaged 16.4 points per game, while averaging 19 points in the playoffs.

In an era of low-scoring games, "Jumpin' Joe" Fulks (right) certainly stood out. Opponents had difficulty slowing down this revolutionary scorer. The three-time All-BAA First Team selection amassed 8,591 points in eight professional seasons.

Center George Mikan was not only the cornerstone of the Minneapolis Lakers dynasty but was also the NBA's first superstar.

The NBA's First Dynasty

Their six titles in seven seasons proved the Minneapolis Lakers' dominance. The Lakers formed as part of the NBL in 1947, and assembled a potent nucleus that would stay in tact all the way to its members' respective inductions into the Basketball Hall of Fame. It featured head coach John Kundla, forwards Jim Pollard and Vern Mikkelsen, and guard Slater Martin, who were joined later by forward/center Clyde Lovellette. The centerpiece of this basketball juggernaut was superstar center George Mikan.

"Mikan ran the whole show," said Larry Foust, the 6-9 center for the Fort Wayne Pistons. "Nobody had better offensive moves under the basket. When George played, he owned that lane."

The 6-10 center was simply superior, winning five consecutive scoring titles and changing the game with his all-around dominance. The Lakers won the NBL crown in their inaugural season, defeating the Rochester Royals in four games, and then jumped to the BAA (renamed the NBA shortly thereafter) to continue their undefeated run. There they won five titles in the next six years and established their role as the NBA's first dynasty.

In his 11 years at the helm of the Minneapolis Lakers, John Kundla compiled a 423–302 record along with six titles.

CHAMPIONSHIP TEAMS

1946–47 Philadelphia Warriors

1947–48 Baltimore Bullets

1948–49 Minneapolis Lakers

1950–1952

AS THE NBA ENTERED the 1950s, change was on the immediate horizon. In the first year of the decade, the league welcomed its first African-American players—Chuck Cooper, Nat "Sweetwater" Clifton, and Earl Lloyd—as well as Bob Cousy and Paul Arizin, a pair of future Hall of Famers who would become icons in their respective cities of Boston and Philadelphia. However, the more things changed, the more they stayed the same, as the Minneapolis Lakers continued their championship run from the 1940s, winning two out of the first three NBA titles of the new decade.

"Pitchin' Paul" Arizin

One of the greatest NBA players of all time did not even make his high-school team. It was the school's loss, however, since Paul Arizin, who joined the Philadelphia Warriors in 1950 and retired as the NBA's third all-time leading scorer in 1962, possessed one of the most picture-perfect jump shots ever seen. "Pitchin' Paul" averaged more than 20 points for nine consecutive campaigns and, after leading the NBA in scoring after his second season, missed two years due to military service. Arizin came back to lead the Warriors to the 1956 NBA championship.

"The Cooz"

The 1950–51 NBA season welcomed one of the greatest point guards to ever play the game. Bob Cousy, the former Holy Cross star, was acquired by Boston in a most unconventional way: his name was drawn out of a hat. Cousy was first drafted in 1950, by the Tri-Cities Blackhawks and then traded to the Chicago Stags, who folded after the 1949–50 season. The Celtics acquired Cousy's rights in a dispersal draft of the Stags franchise. The ballhandling whiz went on to become one of the Celtics most storied players.

In 10 seasons, Paul Arizin led the NBA twice in scoring and was a 10-time All-Star.

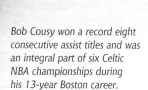

Bob Cousy won a record eight consecutive assist titles and was an integral part of six Celtic NBA championships during his 13-year Boston career.

CHAMPIONSHIP TEAMS

1949–50 Minneapolis Lakers

1950–51 Rochester Royals

1951–52 Minneapolis Lakers

The NBA's African-American Pioneers

Chuck Cooper, Nat "Sweetwater" Clifton, and Earl Lloyd are the NBA's African-American pioneers. These three men entered the NBA prior to the 1950–51 season, and were integral to the evolution of the league.

Four years after the NBA was born, each player made history in his own right. Chuck Cooper became the first African-American to be drafted by an NBA franchise when the Boston Celtics selected the 6-5 forward in the second round of the 1950 NBA Draft.

Also in 1950, Nat Clifton, the 6-6 center for the New York Knickerbockers, became the first African-American to sign an NBA contract.

And on October 31, 1950, as a 6-5 forward for the Washington Capitols, Earl Lloyd made history as the first African-American to step onto an NBA court.

A second-round pick out of Duquesne University, Chuck Cooper (above right) played four seasons for Red Auerbach.

Fort Wayne Whips Celtics in Opener

FORT WAYNE, Ind., Nov. 2 (AP)—The Fort Wayne Pistons cut loose with their fast break in the second half and won a 107-84 victory over the Boston Celtics tonight. Fort Wayne held only a 47-45 lead at the half. It was the opening game of the National Basket Ball Association for each team.

Chuck Cooper scored seven points in his NBA debut against the Fort Wayne Pistons on November 2, 1950.

Nat Clifton enjoyed seven seasons as a valuable player for head coach Joe Lapchick and the New York Knickerbockers.

Earl Lloyd's nine-year NBA career included six with Syracuse, where he helped the Nationals win the 1955 NBA title.

1953–1955

THE MINNEAPOLIS LAKERS' dynasty was drawing to a close by the mid-50s, as new players and teams began to emerge to the forefront. Dolph Schayes of the Syracuse Nationals and Bob Pettit of the St. Louis Hawks, for example, led their teams to multiple NBA Finals appearances, each of them eventually winning a title. Off the court, a man by the name of Danny Biasone invented the 24-second shot clock, which provided the NBA with a much needed shot in the arm by increasing scoring averages considerably.

Syracuse's Favorite Son

The growth and popularity of the NBA received a boost from Dolph Schayes of the Syracuse Nationals. The 6-8 forward/center, who had earned Rookie of the Year honors for the Nationals in the National Basketball League, led the NBA in rebounding in only his second season, after Syracuse joined the new league.

A versatile offensive player, Schayes quickly established himself as one of the NBA's premier stars. He was also an excellent free-throw shooter, leading the league in percentages three times during his career. One of his tricks was to practice free throws on a 14-inch diameter hoop that was nestled within a regulation 18-inch basket.

Schayes led the Nationals to the 1950 and '54 NBA Finals, but the team lost both times to the Minneapolis Lakers. In 1955, Schayes and the Nationals finally broke through, defeating the Fort Wayne Pistons to win the 1955 NBA championship.

Dolph Schayes (right) ascended to a position among the NBA's elite players and enjoyed a Hall-of-Fame career. In 16 seasons, Schayes scored 19,247 points and played in 1,059 games, which was then an NBA record.

Danny Biasone: Reviving the Game

He never logged a minute of NBA action, yet no one had a bigger impact on the game. If it wasn't for Danny Biasone, the professional game of basketball might not have survived.

The NBA in the late 1940s and early '50s featured a style of play that produced primarily low-scoring games. Perhaps the most famous of those was the 19–18 game between the Fort Wayne Pistons and the Minneapolis Lakers, which featured a total of only eight baskets.

Biasone, who was the owner of the Syracuse Nationals, knew the game needed to increase its scoring, so he devised the 24-second shot clock. The idea was that players would be forced to shoot before the 24 seconds expired, compelling teams to shoot more often, and therefore score more often. The clock produced immediate results. Team scoring went up from 79.5 to 93.1 points per game.

"Danny Biasone saved the NBA with the 24-second rule, make no mistake," said former NBA coach and referee Charlie Eckman.

Danny Biasone is also credited with the backcourt rule, which awards two foul shots for backcourt fouls.

The 24-second shot clock made its debut in the 1954–55 season, and has remained a fixture to this day.

Bob Pettit and the St. Louis Hawks

The Hawks called two different locations home before landing in St. Louis in 1955. Originating in the Tri-Cities area as the Blackhawks, the team then moved to Milwaukee for six years, where they acquired their abbreviated name.

Finally, the Hawks made the trip from Milwaukee to St. Louis, where superstar Bob Pettit proceeded to lead them to four NBA Finals appearances over the next six years. The Baton Rouge, Louisiana, native earned NBA Rookie of the Year honors and single-handedly avenged the Hawks' painful seven-game series loss to the Boston Celtics in the 1957 NBA Finals. Pettit scored a single-game Finals record of 58 points in Game 7 of the 1958 Finals, leading St. Louis to the NBA title. In the process, he temporarily interrupted the Celtics run of consecutive championships. St. Louis would later lose to the Celtics in back-to-back Finals series in 1960 and '61.

Bob Pettit (right) was Mr. Hawk. The 6-9 power forward dominated play in the 1950s and '60s. Pettit earned NBA MVP honors in 1956 and '59, and played in 11 straight NBA All-Star Games, picking up three MVP awards.

CHAMPIONSHIP TEAMS

1952–53 Minneapolis Lakers

1953–54 Minneapolis Lakers

1954–55 Syracuse Nationals

1956–1959

AS THE NBA SAID goodbye to the dynasty of the Minneapolis Lakers, it said hello to that of the Celtics. Under the guidance of coach Red Auerbach, the Boston team, which already featured All-Stars Bob Cousy and Bill Sharman, acquired one of the greatest championship cornerstones ever in Bill Russell, whose shotblocking and defensive abilities made a huge impact on the league.

But the Celtic mystique didn't overshadow other great players who were making a mark in their own right, most notably George Yardley and rookie sensation Elgin Baylor, both of whom set new standards for offensive brilliance.

Owner Walter Brown (left) watches as Red Auerbach (center) and the Celtics celebrate their 1957 championship title.

Bill Russell made an immediate impact during his rookie season, leading the NBA in rebounding with 19.6.

Bill Russell: Cornerstone Champ

One of the greatest trades of all time and one that would pay dividends for the next 13 seasons, Bill Russell, who was selected by the St. Louis Hawks in the first round of the 1956 NBA Draft, was soon acquired by Red Auerbach and the Boston Celtics, who knew a defensive force meant championships.

Russell led the University of San Francisco to two NCAA titles, and his NBA debut was delayed because he was helping lead the US to the gold medal in the 1956 Olympics. The wait was well worth it, as Russell and the Celtics won the first of many championships in his rookie season.

A Tradition Is Born

The Boston Celtics' dynasty started to take root after the team's first NBA title in 1957. Thanks to their coach and general manager Red Auerbach, the team was loaded with talent. In one of the most important periods in franchise history, Auerbach acquired three future Hall of Famers via trade or draft in 1956—Bill Russell, Tom Heinsohn, and K. C. Jones. Due to a prior military commitment, Jones didn't join the Celtics until the 1958–59 season, but Russell and Heinsohn fit in nicely with the current nucleus of players led by Bob Cousy and Bill Sharman. Boston won the Eastern Division that season before defeating the St. Louis Hawks in a thrilling seven-game series in the 1957 NBA Finals.

The Celtics' dominance established their popularity throughout the NBA.

The Celtics' first championship went the distance against the St. Louis Hawks in a double-overtime Game 7 classic.

THE BOSTON SUNDAY HERALD SPORTS SECTION

Heinsohn Leads Way with 37 Points, Russell Also Excels

CELTICS TAKE TITLE, 125-123

Ramsey's Goal Shades St. Louis In 2 Overtimes

Pitching Big Sox Question

Infielders Form Better Defense

Yanks, Redlegs Loom as Victors

B'S BACKS AT WALL

The offensive-minded George Yardley scored 9,063 points in seven NBA seasons for a 19.2 average. The six-time All-Star averaged 20.3 in the playoffs.

CHAMPIONSHIP TEAMS

1955–56 Philadelphia Warriors

1956–57 Boston Celtics

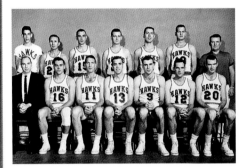

1957–58 St. Louis Hawks

1958–59 Boston Celtics

George Yardley: Scoring Machine

The Fort Wayne Pistons reached the NBA Finals twice in a row in the 1950s, thanks in large part to All-Star George Yardley. The 6-5 jump-shooting forward, who was nicknamed "Yardbird" at Stanford, entered the NBA in 1953, after having served in the military for two seasons. Averaging 9 points during his rookie season, Yardley then averaged 17.3 and 17.4 points while leading the Pistons to their back-to-back Finals appearances, which included a heartbreaking seven-game series loss to the Syracuse Nationals in 1955.

Yardley's best individual season came in 1957–58, when he became the first player in league history to score more than 2,000 points in a season. He scored 2,001 for the Detroit Pistons—surpassing the record of 1,932 held by Minneapolis Laker George Mikan—and earned All-NBA First Team honors after averaging 27.8 points, 10.7 rebounds, and 80 percent from the free-throw line.

Elgin Baylor: Unstoppable Force

The dynasty days were long gone for the Minneapolis Lakers, as the team finished last in the Western Division following the 1957–58 season. The Lakers were in desperate need of a franchise player and certainly found one when they selected Elgin Baylor with the No. 1 overall pick of the 1958 NBA Draft.

The 6-5 high-flying forward made an instant impact with the Lakers, averaging 24.9 points and 15 rebounds on his way to the NBA's Rookie of the Year Award and All-NBA First Team honors. Baylor's arrival marked the revival of the Lakers, who relocated to Los Angeles after his second season. There, the 11-time NBA All-Star enjoyed his greatest statistical campaign, averaging 34.8 points and 19.8 rebounds, once earning 71 points during a single game.

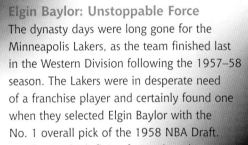

Elgin Baylor was a force throughout his 14-year career, scoring more than 23,000 points.

Individual Honors

1946–47

Scoring Leader:
Joe Fulks, Philadelphia (23.2)

Assist Leader:
Ernie Calverley, Providence (3.4)

Free-Throw Leader:
Fred Scolari, Washington (.811)

1947–48

Scoring Leader:
Joe Fulks, Philadelphia (22.1)

Assist Leader (tie):
Howie Dallmar, Philadelphia and
Ernie Calverley, Providence (2.5)

Free-Throw Leader:
Bob Feerick, Washington (.788)

1948–49

Scoring Leader:
George Mikan, Minneapolis (28.3)

Assist Leader:
Bob Davies, Rochester (5.4)

Free-Throw Leader:
Bob Feerick (.859)

1949–50

Scoring Leader:
George Mikan, Minneapolis (27.4)

Assist Leader:
Andy Phillip, Chicago (5.8)

Free-Throw Leader:
Max Zaslofsky, Chicago (.843)

1950–51

Scoring Leader:
George Mikan, Minneapolis (28.4)

Rebound Leader:
Dolph Schayes, Syracuse (16.4)

Assist Leader (tie):
Andy Phillip, Philadelphia and
Dick McGuire, New York (6.3)

Free-Throw Leader:
Joe Fulks, Philadelphia (.855)

1951–52

Scoring Leader:
Paul Arizin, Philadelphia (25.4)

Rebound Leader:
George Mikan, Minneapolis (13.5)

Assist Leader:
Andy Phillip, Philadelphia (8.2)

Free-Throw Leader:
Bobby Wanzer, Rochester (.904)

1952–53

Scoring Leader:
Neil Johnston, Philadelphia (22.3)

Rebound Leader:
George Mikan, Minneapolis (14.4)

Assist Leader:
Bob Cousy, Boston (7.7)

Free-Throw Leader:
Bill Sharman, Boston (.850)

Rookie of the Year:
Don Meineke, Fort Wayne

1953–54

Scoring Leader:
Neil Johnston, Philadelphia (24.4)

Rebound Leader:
Harry Gallatin, New York (15.3)

Assist Leader:
Bob Cousy, Boston (7.2)

Free-Throw Leader:
Bill Sharman, Boston (.844)

Rookie of the Year:
Ray Felix, Baltimore

1954–55

Scoring Leader:
Neil Johnston, Philadelphia (22.7)

Rebound Leader:
Neil Johnston, Philadelphia (15.1)

Assist Leader:
Bob Cousy, Boston (7.9)

Free-Throw Leader:
Bill Sharman, Boston (.897)

Rookie of the Year:
Bob Pettit, Milwaukee

1955–56

Scoring Leader:
Bob Pettit, St. Louis (25.7)

Rebound Leader:
Maurice Stokes, Rochester (16.3)

Assist Leader:
Bob Cousy, Boston (8.9)

Free-Throw Leader:
Bill Sharman, Boston (.867)

MVP: Bob Pettit, St. Louis

Rookie of the Year:
Maurice Stokes, Rochester

1956–57

Scoring Leader:
Paul Arizin, Philadelphia (25.6)

Rebound Leader:
Maurice Stokes, Rochester (17.4)

Assist Leader:
Bob Cousy, Boston (7.5)

Free-Throw Leader:
Bill Sharman, Boston (.905)

MVP: Bob Cousy, Boston

Rookie of the Year:
Tom Heinsohn, Boston

1957–58

Scoring Leader:
George Yardley, Detroit (27.8)

Rebound Leader:
Bill Russell, Boston (22.7)

Assist Leader:
Bob Cousy, Boston (7.1)

Free-Throw Leader:
Dolph Schayes, Syracuse (.904)

MVP: Bill Russell, Boston

Rookie of the Year:
Woody Sauldsberry, Philadelphia

1958–59

Scoring Leader:
Bob Pettit, St. Louis (29.2)

Rebound Leader:
Bill Russell, Boston (23.0)

Assist Leader:
Bob Cousy, Boston (8.6)

Free-Throw Leader:
Bill Sharman, Boston (.932)

MVP: Bob Pettit, St. Louis

Rookie of the Year:
Elgin Baylor, Minneapolis

Hall of Fame Class:
The First Team, Team
Original Celtics, Team
Forrest Clare Allen, Coach
Henry Clifford Carlson, Coach
Dr. Luther Gulick, Contributor
Edward J. Hickox, Contributor
Charles D. Hyatt, Player
Matthew P. Kennedy, Referee
Angelo Luisetti, Player
Walter E. Meanwell, M.D., Coach
George L. Mikan, Player
Ralph Morgan, Contributor
Dr. James Naismith, Contributor
Harold G. Olsen, Contributor
John J. Schommer, Player
Amos Alonzo Stagg, Contributor
Oswald Tower, Contributor

1960–1962

The early '60s were exciting years for basketball. As Red Auerbach and the Boston Celtics continued their unprecedented series of championship wins, 1960 saw the arrival of three of the NBA's most spectacular rookies—Oscar Robertson, Jerry West, and Lenny Wilkens. Then in 1962, the unthinkable happened: Philadelphia Warrior Wilt Chamberlain scored 100 points in one game—a record which stands unbroken to this day.

Jerry West: Driven to Perfection

Jerry West's basketball résumé sparkled well before the Lakers selected him with the No. 2 overall pick in the 1960 NBA Draft. The 6-2 shooting guard led his high-school team to a state title, his West Virginia college team to the 1959 NCAA Championship Game, and, despite losing, still earned NCAA Tournament Most Outstanding Player honors.

West, along with Oscar Robertson, then led the US Olympic Team to the gold medal in the 1960 Games in Rome. So it was little surprise that the 6-2 guard enjoyed one of the greatest careers in NBA history.

What separated him from other great players was not only his ability to deliver in the clutch, but also his intense approach to the game, which became as much of a trademark as his flashy statistics. West is the Lakers' all-time leading scorer with 25,192 points.

THE BIG O'S TRIPLE-DOUBLE SPECTACULAR

The Cincinnati Royals selected Oscar Robertson, the 6-5 All-America guard and three-time College Player of the Year, with their 1960 territorial draft choice, and he certainly didn't disappoint. Robertson dominated in his rookie season, averaging 30.5 points, 10.1 rebounds, and 9.7 assists on his way to NBA Rookie of the Year honors. What would Robertson do for an encore? Try 30.8 points, 12.5 rebounds, and 11.4 assists—a triple-double. Robertson is the only player in NBA history to accomplish such a feat. Robertson was so good that he actually averaged a triple-double during his first five NBA seasons.

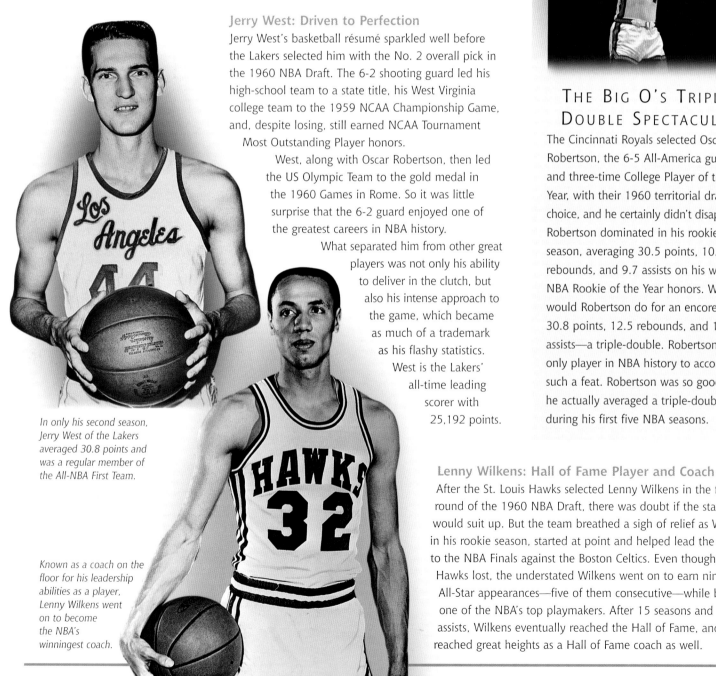

In only his second season, Jerry West of the Lakers averaged 30.8 points and was a regular member of the All-NBA First Team.

Known as a coach on the floor for his leadership abilities as a player, Lenny Wilkens went on to become the NBA's winningest coach.

Lenny Wilkens: Hall of Fame Player and Coach

After the St. Louis Hawks selected Lenny Wilkens in the first round of the 1960 NBA Draft, there was doubt if the star guard would suit up. But the team breathed a sigh of relief as Wilkens, in his rookie season, started at point and helped lead the Hawks to the NBA Finals against the Boston Celtics. Even though the Hawks lost, the understated Wilkens went on to earn nine NBA All-Star appearances—five of them consecutive—while becoming one of the NBA's top playmakers. After 15 seasons and 7,211 assists, Wilkens eventually reached the Hall of Fame, and later reached great heights as a Hall of Fame coach as well.

CHAMPIONSHIP TEAMS

1959–60 Boston Celtics

1960–61 Boston Celtics

1961–62 Boston Celtics

Wilt Hits The Century Mark

Only 4,124 people witnessed the greatest individual scoring performance in NBA history on March 2, 1962, when Wilt Chamberlain put on basketball's ultimate one-man show, scoring 100 points in a single game as the Philadelphia Warriors defeated the New York Knicks 169–147. Chamberlain sliced through New York's defense with an awesome array of inside power moves and perimeter shots that overwhelmed the Knicks to the tune of 41 first-half points. When the second-year player scored 28 points in the third quarter, running his game total to 69, Chamberlain was on course to break the single-game scoring mark of 78 points—a mark he had set two months earlier.

Swelling in anticipation, fans chanted, "We want 100!" The Warriors' announcer Dave Zinkoff added to the state of euphoria by starting to announce Chamberlain's point total from the time he scored the 79th historic point. With less than one minute remaining, Warrior Joe Ruklick passed to Chamberlain, who broke free toward the basket and hit the century mark—100 points. Fans and photographers stormed the floor.

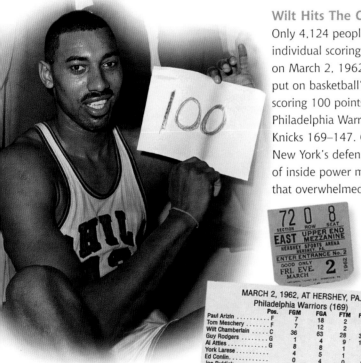

Wilt Chamberlain displays his point total from March 2, 1962—the highest score ever achieved by one player in a game.

One of the few mementos that remain from Wilt Chamberlain's historic 100-point game is this rare ticket stub. The Philadelphia Warriors played this home game in Hershey, Pennsylvania.

MARCH 2, 1962, AT HERSHEY, PA.
Philadelphia Warriors (169)

	Pos.	FGM	FGA	FTM	FTA	Pts.
Paul Arizin	F	7	18	2	2	16
Tom Meschery	F	7	12	2	2	16
Wilt Chamberlain	C	36	63	28	32	100
Guy Rodgers	G	1	4	9	12	11
Al Attles	G	8	8	1	1	17
York Larese		4	5	1	1	9
Ed Conlin		0	4	0	0	0
Joe Ruklick		0	1	0	2	0
Ted Luckenbill		0	0	0	0	0
Totals		63	115	43	52	169

FG pct.: .548. FT pct.: .827. Team rebounds: 3.

Red Auerbach lights up a cigar and celebrates another title for the Boston Celtics.

The Championship Architect

The 1960s unfolded as a decade of great social change, yet even though the NBA would grow as a league, some things seemed to stay the same—such as the Boston Celtics winning championships year after year. After a springboard championship defeat of the Minneapolis Lakers in the 1959 NBA Finals, the Celtics rolled off seven straight championships in the '60s, bowing only once—to Wilt Chamberlain and the 1966–67 Philadelphia 76ers in the conference finals—before reaching the end of the decade.

The architect and mastermind of this basketball juggernaut was Arnold "Red" Auerbach, the Celtics' aggressive, cigar-chomping head coach, who, through shrewd trades and stellar coaching, was responsible for an unprecedented run of nine championships in 10 seasons (1959–66).

1963–1966

CHAMBERLAIN VERSUS RUSSELL. It was a match-up that not only elevated the league's popularity but redefined the term "rivalry." Their decade-long duel captivated NBA fans everywhere with its epic battles. Meanwhile, Boston Celtic John Havlicek helped his team hold on to their championship run as he made an infamous steal during the 1965 Eastern Conference Finals. And as the Celtics rampaged on throughout the '60s, their mighty coach Red Auerbach closed out his brilliant coaching career with the Celtics in typical Red style—with another championship.

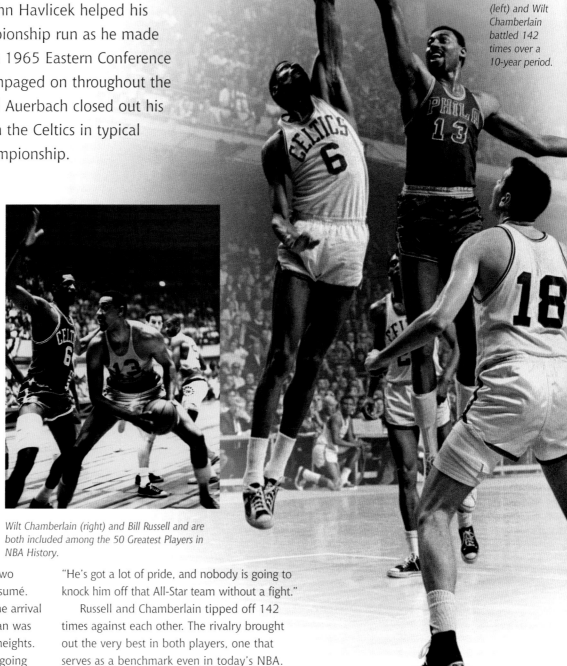

Bill Russell (left) and Wilt Chamberlain battled 142 times over a 10-year period.

The NBA's Greatest Individual Rivalry

It was a classic confrontation: the greatest scoring force in the game versus the most dominant defensive stopper. Although Wilt Chamberlain had better numbers (28.7 points and 28.7 rebounds compared to Bill Russell's 14.5 and 23.7), the Celtic great enjoyed a one-sided advantage when it came to championships—winning nine titles during a 10-year span. In the 1960s, it seemed like no team in the NBA, let alone the Eastern Conference, could slow down the Celtics' dynasty. The one team that did was Wilt's: the '67 Sixers.

When Chamberlain joined the Philadelphia Warriors prior to the 1959–60 season, Russell had already established himself as one of the league's premier players, with two championships and counting on his résumé. Players around the league knew that the arrival of the University of Kansas All-American was going to push Russell to even greater heights.

"This challenge by Chamberlain is going to make [Russell] better than ever," said Carl Braun, a former New York Knicks guard.

Wilt Chamberlain (right) and Bill Russell and are both included among the 50 Greatest Players in NBA History.

"He's got a lot of pride, and nobody is going to knock him off that All-Star team without a fight."

Russell and Chamberlain tipped off 142 times against each other. The rivalry brought out the very best in both players, one that serves as a benchmark even in today's NBA.

"People say it was the greatest individual rivalry they've ever seen," said Russell. "I agree."

"If I had my back turned I never would have been able to see the ball," John Havlicek explained about his game-winning clutch move.

1962–63 Boston Celtics

1963–64 Boston Celtics

1964–65 Boston Celtics

1965–66 Boston Celtics

Havlicek Stole the Ball!

The first-round pick of the 1962 NBA Draft out of Ohio State was joining a dynasty in the making. When John Havlicek arrived in Boston, the Celtics were on a championship roll, having just won four in a row. Havlicek, whether playing as sixth man or starter, eventually contributed to eight more titles before he would end his Hall of Fame career. Yet, despite enjoying one of the most accomplished runs in NBA history, the Celtics' all-time leading scorer is perhaps most

remembered for one of the greatest clutch plays in NBA Playoff history. The scene: Game 7 of the 1965 Eastern Conference Finals. The opponent: Philadelphia 76ers. The stakes: winner advances to the NBA Finals.

With the Celtics clinging to a 110–109 lead, the 76ers had a golden opportunity for the game-winning shot. With seconds left in regulation, Hal Greer inbounded the ball and threw a lob to his teammate Chet Walker. With the sellout Boston Garden crowd on their feet in eager anticipation, Havlicek, who had one eye on the ball and one eye on Walker, suddenly reached out and deflected the ball to his teammate Sam Jones. The Garden erupted. The Celtics dynasty stayed intact and the momentum from that series helped secure the franchise's seventh consecutive title.

This One's For You, Red

The mighty Celtics finally showed signs of vulnerability: after winning a record nine Eastern Division consecutive titles, they finished second to the Philadelphia 76ers. But they ended any premature talk of their demise by defeating the Sixers in the 1966 Eastern Division Finals. Only the Los Angeles Lakers stood in the way of Red Auerbach and the Celtics earning their record ninth Finals title.

The Lakers were eager to take on a team they had lost to in three of the four previous NBA Finals. Fueling the belief that it was their

year, the Lakers defeated the Celtics 133–129 in Game 1. But the win was overshadowed when Auerbach announced his retirement during the postgame, adding that Bill Russell, the Celtics All-Star center, would replace him. The news shook up the basketball world and unnerved the Lakers. Boston went on to win the series and Auerbach retired on top.

Bill Russell and Red Auerbach celebrate their 1966 NBA championship win, the Celtics' eighth in a row.

1966–1968

THE BOSTON CELTICS' championship run was over—or rather, it was taking a breather. Boston's string of eight straight NBA titles finally ended, thanks to the dominance of Wilt Chamberlain and the 1967 Philadelphia 76ers. The Chamberlain–Russell rivalry would come to a head as the Sixers displayed a balanced attack, led by Chamberlain and coached by Alex Hannum.

While the NBA crowned a new champion, it also saw the arrival of a new league, the American Basketball Association, which eventually loomed as a threat to secure top talent.

CHAMBERLAIN'S CHAMPIONSHIP MISSION

After only seven years in the league, Wilt Chamberlain achieved many individual records, including a 100-point game, an average of 50.4 points per game during the 1961–62 season, and two NBA MVPs. The one accolade that eluded the 7-1 All-Star center was an NBA championship.

Chamberlain started the 1964–65 season with the Philadelphia 76ers. The arrival of his former coach, Alex Hannum, prior to the 1966–67 season helped change the approach of the game's most dominant player. Under Hannum's guidance, Chamberlain learned to play a more efficient game, altering to a more team-oriented style. He took 840 fewer field-goal attempts, averaging 24.1 points (nine less than the previous season but still earning a record .683 field-goal percentage). He also averaged 7.8 assists, a career high, which ranked third in the league that season.

Record Season

The Sixers now featured a balanced attack with six players averaging in double figures— Chamberlain (24.1), Hal Greer (22.10), Chet Walker (19.3), Billy Cunningham (18.5), Wali Jones (13.2), and Lucious Jackson (12.0)— establishing an NBA record 68-13 regular-season mark, while averaging 125.2 points

The Philadelphia 76ers celebrate their 1967 NBA championship title, breaking the Celtics' stranglehold over the rest of the NBA.

per game. Chamberlain's all-around game netted him his third MVP award.

Perhaps most gratifying for Chamberlain was that he would finally defeat his longtime rival Bill Russell. The Sixers brought the Boston Celtics' record run of eight championships in a row to a halt when they defeated them in five games in the Eastern Division Finals.

The Sixers went on to upend the San Francisco Warriors in six games in the NBA Finals. The championship was significant as Hannum became the first coach in NBA history to lead two teams to titles (he had taken St. Louis to victory in 1958), while Chamberlain finally reached the status he had long coveted: NBA champion.

FINAL STANDINGS

EASTERN DIVISION

	Phi.	Bos.	Cin.	N.Y.	Balt.	S.F.	St.L.	L.A.	Chi.	Det.	W	L	Pct.	GB
Philadelphia	..	4	8	8	8	7	8	8	8	9	68	13	.840	—
Boston	5	..	8	9	8	6	5	5	8	6	60	21	.741	8
Cincinnati	1	1	..	6	6	5	6	3	4	7	39	42	.481	29
New York	1	0	3	..	7	5	4	5	6	5	36	45	.444	32
Baltimore	1	1	3	2	..	2	4	2	3	2	20	61	.247	48

WESTERN DIVISION

	Phi.	Bos.	Cin.	N.Y.	Balt.	S.F.	St.L.	L.A.	Chi.	Det.	W	L	Pct.	GB
San Francisco	2	3	4	4	7	..	5	6	6	7	44	37	.543	—
St. Louis	1	4	3	5	5	4	..	5	5	7	39	42	.481	5
Los Angeles	1	4	6	4	7	3	4	..	3	3	36	45	.444	8
Chicago	1	1	5	3	6	3	4	6	..	4	33	48	.407	11
Detroit	0	3	2	4	7	2	2	5	5	..	30	51	.370	14

CHAMPIONSHIP TEAMS

1966–67 Philadelphia 76ers

1967–68 Boston Celtics

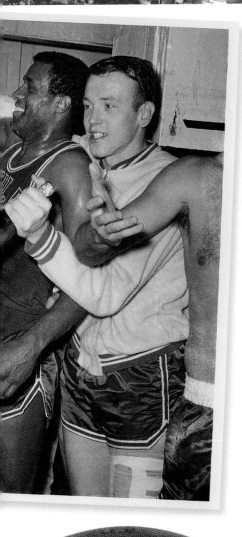

THE ABA'S FIRST STAR

A tremendous leaper, Connie Hawkins was a free-wheeling force who led the new league in scoring in its inaugural season with a 26.8 points-per-page average, while also pulling down 13.5 rebounds per game. The 6-5, 215-pound forward led the Pittsburgh Pipers to an Eastern Division title and the league's first championship.

Hawkins, who had previously played with the American Basketball League and the Harlem Globetrotters, arrived in the ABA when he was denied admission to the NBA after being associated with a college basketball scandal at the University of Iowa. Never convicted, Hawkins joined the NBA and the Phoenix Suns in the 1969–70 season.

The ABA's symbol—a red, white, and blue ball—was unmistakable, and so was the league's spirit, which featured a three-point line, an uptempo style of play, and plenty of high-flying dunks.

Connie Hawkins followed the great Elgin Baylor in the ultra-exclusive line of high flyers, and demonstrated those skills on a nightly basis to the oohs and aahs of ABA fans everywhere.

ABA: A NEW LEAGUE IN TOWN

The American Basketball Association officially formed on February 1, 1967, featuring 11 teams throughout the United States, ranging from Anaheim, Kentucky, to Pittsburgh, Pennsylvania, and its impact can still be felt to this day. The league would eventually serve as the launching pad for some of the NBA's greatest players—Connie Hawkins, Spencer Haywood, Moses Malone, Julius Erving, George Gervin, David Thompson, and Dan Issel—while a host of others, such as Rick Barry, Billy Cunningham, and George McGinnis, tested their skills in both leagues.

The ABA's first commissioner was George Mikan, the former NBA All-Star center who led the Minneapolis Lakers to six titles. The Pittsburgh Pipers earned the distinction of the first ABA champions. As the decade drew to a close, not only was the ABA alive and well—it was competing against the NBA for top senior collegiate talent. It wasn't long before the NBA began to take serious notice.

1968–1969

AS THE 1960S DREW TO A CLOSE, so did the celebrated dynasty of the Boston Celtics, who won their 11th title in 13 seasons. Bill Russell, one of the NBA's most accomplished and dominant players, retired following the 1968–69 season, after winning 11 championships, more than any other player in NBA history. While the NBA said goodbye to one legend, it welcomed several new ones—Dave Bing, Elvin Hayes, and Wes Unseld—three players who excelled in their rookie seasons on their way to distinguished Hall of Fame careers.

Dave Bing: Mr. Piston

It wasn't the most impressive rookie debut, but it was one of the most memorable. Dave Bing, the No. 2 pick of the 1966 NBA Draft, missed his first six shots as a member of the Detroit Pistons, and went scoreless for the first time in his basketball career. Fortunately, for Bing and Pistons fans, this wasn't indicative of things to come. Bing, the 6-3 All-American out of Syracuse, went on to win 1967 NBA Rookie of the Year honors, averaging 20 points per game, en route to becoming only the sixth first-year player in NBA history to score more than 1,600 points. The next season, Bing made history as he became the first guard since Max Zaslofsky of the BAA's Chicago Stags to lead the league in scoring, when he averaged 27.1 points per game. Bing was so dominant that season, he even unseated the great Jerry West from the All-NBA First Team spot.

1968–69 Boston Celtics

Dave Bing starred for the Detroit Pistons for nine seasons before being traded to the Washington Bullets in 1975.

Elvin Hayes (left) ended his career third all-time in points (27,313) and rebounds (16,279), and first in games played (1,303) and minutes (50,000). Wes Unseld (right) played 13 seasons for the Bullets, averaging more than 10 rebounds in 12 seasons.

Elvin Hayes and Wes Unseld: Instant Impacts

The 1968–69 season may have marked the beginning of the end of the Celtics dynasty, but it also served as an introduction to new greatness. The NBA welcomed two rookies—Elvin Hayes of the San Diego Rockets and Wes Unseld of the Washington Bullets—who dominated play in their first season. Hayes, a 6-9 power forward/center out of the University of Houston, led the NBA in several categories—scoring (28.4), points (2,327), minutes (3,695), as well as field goals made (930) and attempted (2,083). Unseld, a bruising 6-7 power forward out of the University of Louisville, joined Wilt Chamberlain as the only player to win the NBA's Rookie of the Year and NBA MVP Award in the same season. He averaged 13.8 points and 18.2 rebounds, helping the Bullets win the Eastern Division with a 57-25 record.

CHAMPIONSHIP TEAM

Championship Greatness

When Bill Russell assumed the coaching duties from legendary Red Auerbach following the 1965–66 season, the 6-10 center made history as the first African-American coach in major-league professional sports. Russell, who would serve three years as a player-coach for the Boston Celtics, had the daunting task of sustaining the NBA's greatest dynasty. In his first season, the Celtics' championship streak came to an end when Wilt Chamberlain and the Philadeliphia 76ers, owners of the best regular-season record in the NBA (68-13), defeated Boston in five games during the Eastern Division Finals. Not to be deterred, Russell got his revenge the following season when the Celtics defeated the Sixers in six games during a playoff rematch and advanced to the 1968 NBA Finals to defeat the Los Angeles Lakers in another six games. After taking the crown once again in 1969 (see below), Russell retired on top.

No player has won more NBA Finals series than Bill Russell.

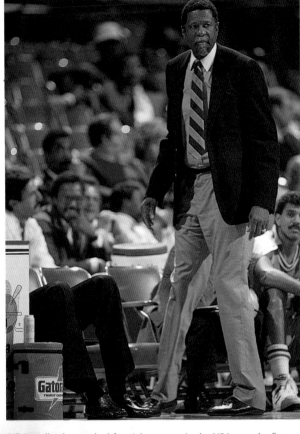

Bill Russell, who coached for eight seasons in the NBA, was the first African-American coach to win a professional championship.

Lakers–Celtics Rivalry

The Celtics barely made the playoffs in the 1968–69 season, but still managed to advance to the NBA Finals opposite the Los Angeles Lakers—again. Wilt Chamberlain, who was acquired by L.A. before the season began, battled Russell and the Celtics for seven games before Boston emerged victorious. For the Lakers, it was another heartbreaking loss to the Celtics, their sixth Finals setback in that decade. Russell retired following that season, winning his second championship as a player-coach, which capped off a brilliant career that included five NBA MVPs and 11 championships in 13 seasons.

The Boston Celtics and the Los Angeles Lakers went head-to-head in six NBA Finals over a 10-year period during the 1960s.

Individual Honors

1959–60

Scoring Leader:
Wilt Chamberlain,
Philadelphia (37.6)
Rebound Leader:
Wilt Chamberlain,
Philadelphia (27.0)
Assist Leader:
Bob Cousy, Boston (9.5)
Free-Throw Leader:
Dolph Schayes, Syracuse (.893)
MVP: Wilt Chamberlain,
Philadelphia
Rookie of the Year:
Wilt Chamberlain, Philadelphia
Hall of Fame Class:
Ernest A. Blood, Coach
Victor A. Hanson, Player
George T. Hepbron, Referee
Frank W. Keaney, Coach
Ward L. Lambert, Coach
Edward C. Macauley, Player
Branch McCracken, Player
Charles C. Murphy, Player
Henry V. Porter, Contributor
John R. Wooden, Player

1960–61

Scoring Leader:
Wilt Chamberlain,
Philadelphia (38.4)
Rebound Leader:
Wilt Chamberlain,
Philadelphia (27.2)
Assist Leader:
Oscar Robertson, Cincinnati (9.7)
Free-Throw Leader:
Bill Sharman, Boston (.921)
MVP: Bill Russell, Boston
Rookie of the Year:
Oscar Robertson, Cincinnati
Hall of Fame Class:
Buffalo Germans, Team
Bernard Borgmann, Player
Forrest S. DeBernardi, Player

George H. Hoyt, Referee
George E. Keogan, Coach
Robert A. Kurland, Player
John J. O'Brien, Contributor
Andy Phillip, Player
Ernest C. Quigley, Referee
John S. Roosma, Player
Leonard D. Sachs, Coach
Arthur A. Schabinger, Contributor
Christian Steinmetz, Player
David Tobey, Referee
Arthur L. Trester, Contributor
Edward A. Wachter, Player
David H. Walsh, Referee

1961–62

Scoring Leader:
Wilt Chamberlain,
Philadelphia (50.4)
Rebound Leader:
Wilt Chamberlain,
Philadelphia (25.7)
Assist Leader:
Oscar Robertson, Cincinnati (11.4)
Free-Throw Leader:
Dolph Schayes, Syracuse (.897)
MVP: Bill Russell, Boston
Rookie of the Year:
Walt Bellamy, Chicago
Hall of Fame Class:
Jack McCracken, Player
Frank Morgenweck, Contributor
Harlan O. Page, Player
Barney Sedran, Player
Lynn W. St. John, Contributor
John A. Thompson, Player

1962–63

Scoring Leader:
Wilt Chamberlain,
San Francisco (44.8)
Rebound Leader:
Wilt Chamberlain,
San Francisco (24.3)

Assist Leader:
Guy Rodgers, San Francisco (10.4)
Free-Throw Leader:
Larry Costello, Syracuse (.881)
MVP: Bill Russell, Boston
Rookie of the Year:
Terry Dischinger, Chicago
Coach of the Year:
Harry Gallatin, St. Louis
Hall of Fame Class:
New York Rens, Team
Robert F. Gruenig, Player
William A. Reid, Contributor

1963–64

Scoring Leader:
Wilt Chamberlain,
San Francisco
(36.9)
Rebound Leader:
Bill Russell,
Boston (24.7)
Assist Leader:
Oscar Robertson,
Cincinnati (11.0)
Free-Throw Leader:
Oscar Robertson, Cincinnati (.853)
MVP: Oscar Robertson, Cincinnati
Rookie of the Year:
Jerry Lucas, Cincinnati
Coach of the Year:
Alex Hannum, San Francisco
Hall of Fame Class:
John W. Bunn, Contributor
Harold E. Foster, Player
Nat Holman, Player
Edward S. Irish, Contributor
R. William Jones, Contributor
Kenneth D. Loeffler, Coach
John D. Russell, Player

1964–65

Scoring Leader:
Wilt Chamberlain, San Francisco/Philadelphia (34.7)
Rebound Leader:
Bill Russell, Boston (24.1)
Assist Leader:
Oscar Robertson, Cincinnati (11.5)
Free-Throw Leader:
Larry Costello, Philadelphia (.877)
MVP: Bill Russell, Boston

Rookie of the Year:
Willis Reed, New York
Coach of the Year:
Red Auerbach, Boston
Hall of Fame Class:
Walter A. Brown, Contributor
Paul D. Hinkle, Contributor
Howard A. Hobson, Coach
William G. Mokray, Contributor

1965–66

Scoring Leader:
Wilt Chamberlain, Philadelphia (33.5)
Rebound Leader:
Wilt Chamberlain, Philadelphia (24.6)
Assist Leader:
Oscar Robertson, Cincinnati (11.1)
Free-Throw Leader:
Larry Siegfried, Boston (.881)
MVP: Wilt Chamberlain, Philadelphia
Rookie of the Year:
Rick Barry, San Francisco
Coach of the Year:
Dolph Schayes, Philadelphia
Hall of Fame Class:
Everett S. Dean, Coach
Joe Lapchick, Player

1966–67

Scoring Leader:
Rick Barry, San Francisco (35.6)
Rebound Leader:
Wilt Chamberlain, Philadelphia (24.2)
Assist Leader:
Guy Rodgers, Chicago (11.2)
Free-Throw Leader:
Adrian Smith, Cincinnati (.903)
MVP: Wilt Chamberlain, Philadelphia
Rookie of the Year:
Dave Bing, Detroit
Coach of the Year:
Johnny Kerr, Chicago
Hall of Fame Class:
No enshrinees

1967–68

Scoring Leader:
Dave Bing, Detroit (27.1)
Rebound Leader:
Wilt Chamberlain, Philadelphia (23.8)
Assist Leader:
Oscar Robertson, Cincinnati (9.7)
Free-Throw Leader:
Oscar Robertson, Cincinnati (.873)
MVP: Wilt Chamberlain, Philadelphia
Rookie of the Year:
Earl Monroe, Baltimore
Coach of the Year:
Richie Guerin, St. Louis
Hall of Fame Class:
Clair F. Bee, Contributor
Howard G. Cann, Coach
Amory T. Gill, Coach
Alvin F. Julian, Coach

1968–69

Scoring Leader:
Elvin Hayes, San Diego (28.4)
Rebound Leader:
Wilt Chamberlain, Los Angeles (21.1)
Assist Leader:
Oscar Robertson, Cincinnati (9.8)
Free-Throw Leader:
Larry Siegfried, Boston (.864)
MVP: Wes Unseld, Baltimore
Rookie of the Year:
Wes Unseld, Baltimore
Coach of the Year:
Gene Shue, Baltimore
NBA Finals MVP:
Jerry West, Los Angeles
Hall of Fame Class:
Arnold J. Auerbach, Coach
Henry G. Dehnert, Player
Henry P. Iba, Coach
Adolph F. Rupp, Coach
Charles H. Taylor, Contributor

1970–1972

WHO WOULD CLAIM THE TOP SPOT in the NBA now that the Boston Celtics' dynasty had ended? The New York Knicks stepped forward, winning the decade's first title in dramatic fashion. Meanwhile, Milwaukee acquired perennial All-Star Oscar Robertson, and the future Hall of Famer, along with rising superstar Kareem Abdul-Jabbar, led the Bucks to the 1971 title. The next year, the Lakers won their first title since moving to Los Angeles in 1960. Off the court, the free-agency landscape changed forever when Spencer Haywood successfully challenged the "four-year rule."

"When Willis came out onto the court," said former Knick Bill Bradley. "It was like the place exploded. Chills were going up and down everyone's spine."

FREE-AGENCY PIONEER

Spencer Haywood was the ABA's 1971 Rookie of the Year. Skipping the draft, he signed a six-year NBA contract with the Seattle SuperSonics in 1970, breaking the NBA's policy of not signing players before their classes graduated. The NBA took Haywood and the Sonics to court, where a judge ruled that the NBA's four-year rule was in conflict of the Sherman Antitrust Act. Haywood and the Sonics scored a monumental victory that changed basketball forever.

Drama at the Garden

One year after the end of the Celtics' dynasty, the New York Knicks won a team-record of 18 consecutive games on their way to a franchise-best 60-22 regular-season record. Head coach Red Holzman preached a pressure-defense, teamwork approach, which was embraced by such selfless players as Willis Reed, Clyde Frazier, Bill Bradley, Dave DeBusschere, and Dick Barnett.

New York faced an early playoff test against the Baltimore Bullets, which featured All-Stars Wes Unseld, Earl "The Pearl" Monroe, Gus Johnson, and Jack Marin. In Game 1, the Knicks needed triple overtime to take a 1-0 lead in a series that took them a full seven games to win.

The Knicks had an easier time against the Milwaukee Bucks in the Eastern Division Finals, winning in five games and advancing to the NBA Finals against the Los Angeles Lakers.

The teams split the first four games, with two going into overtime before Willis, the Knicks' All-Star center, suffered a torn muscle in his right leg in Game 5, forcing him to miss Game 6, which the Lakers won in Los Angeles. As the series shifted to New York, everyone wondered if Willis would suit up and play.

One of the most dramatic moments in playoff history unfolded when Reed slowly emerged onto the court as the sold-out Garden crowd went delirious. Willis scored the first two baskets of the game, but his mere presence served as inspiration for the Knicks to win the championship.

The 1970–71 Milwaukee Bucks: From Expansion to Champion

Oscar Robertson's all-around game routinely produced triple-doubles (see page 34) as "The Big O" collected multiple honors over the years. Yet he was missing an NBA championship—but this soon changed when he was traded to the Milwaukee Bucks prior to the 1970–71 season. At age 32, Robertson joined a team that was entering only its third year of existence and featured reigning NBA Rookie of the Year Kareem Abdul-Jabbar, who had averaged 28.8 points while leading the Bucks to 56 wins in the 1969–70 season.

Milwaukee also acquired veterans Lucius Allen and Bob Boozer to complement the existing core group of Bob Dandridge and Jon McGlocklin. Head coach Larry Costello, who took over the expansion Bucks in 1968 following his retirement as a player, guided Milwaukee to an NBA high of 66 regular-season games. Abdul-Jabbar (31.7) and Robertson (19.7) combined for 51.4 points per game as the Bucks leveled the San Francisco Warriors and Los Angeles Lakers in five games each in the Western Conference Playoffs. The Bucks continued their roll when they swept the Baltimore Bullets in five games for the NBA title.

"Larry, Oscar, and I have the same way," Abdul-Jabbar said. "We agree that being as efficient as possible cuts down on our chances for errors."

There were none in that championship season.

After 11 NBA seasons, Oscar Robertson's Hall of Fame résumé was complete after he led the Milwaukee Bucks to the 1971 NBA title. The former Rookie of the Year and MVP set the standard for all-around excellence.

CHAMPIONSHIP TEAMS

1969–70 New York Knicks

1970–71 Milwaukee Bucks

1971–72 Los Angeles Lakers

Gail Goodrich and Jerry West (above center) were the Lakers' top two scorers—the team outscored opponents by an average of 12.3 points per game.

The 1971–72 Los Angeles Lakers: Rolling to Greatness

The championship road was a long one for Jerry West, one of the NBA's greatest players: 12 seasons, 12 NBA All-Star appearances, 832 regular-season games, 135 playoff games, and 8 NBA Finals appearances. Finally, the Lakers broke through and made a convincing case as one of the greatest teams ever. Coached by former Boston Celtics great Bill Sharman and featuring the 35-year-old Wilt Chamberlain and the 33-year-old West, they set an NBA record with 69 regular-season wins, including a record 33 in a row.

The Lakers met the New York Knicks in the Finals, the team that defeated them in 1970. Los Angeles was in no mood for a repeat performance, and defeated the Knicks, who played without Willis Reed, in five games as Chamberlain earned Finals MVP honors.

West's fate then came full circle. The Lakers battled the Knicks in the Finals again the following season only to lose in five games. West retired after the following year.

1973–1975

VIRTUOSO PERFORMANCES took center stage in both the ABA and NBA during the mid-70s. Julius Erving led this creative revolution with his gravity-defying moves, taking the ABA's New York Nets to titles in 1974 and '76, and earning ABA MVP honors in both years. In the NBA, Nate "Tiny" Archibald proved that heart, not height, was the best barometer to judge talent as the 6-1 point guard dominated competition with his scoring and play-making abilities. The underdog role perfectly suited the Golden State Warriors as they shocked the basketball world in upsetting the heavily favored Washington Bullets in the 1975 NBA Finals. Meanwhile, off the court, the first collective bargaining agreement between owners and players brought much needed stability to the game.

JULIUS ERVING TAKES FLIGHT

The perfect premier attraction in a league that celebrated individual virtuosity, innovation, and a relentless up-tempo style of play, Julius Erving entered the ABA with little fanfare only to emerge as the league's most important figure. The 6-7 forward made an instant impact with the Virginia Squires, averaging 27.3 points and 15.7 rebounds in his rookie season, and amazing fans with gravity-defying moves punctuated by rim-rattling dunks.

"I went from doing it by the book in college to having the chains taken off and having the freedom to explore, experiment, dare to be great," said Erving.

And great he was. In his five ABA seasons, two with the Squires and three with the New York Nets, Erving averaged 28.7 points and tallied three scoring titles and two league championships. Erving's out-of-this world talent also played a major role in having four ABA teams, including the Nets, join the NBA in 1976. The man nicknamed "Dr. J" left an indelible mark on a league whose spirit persists to this day.

TINY ARCHIBALD: LITTLE BIG MAN

When 6-1, 160-pound Nate "Tiny" Archibald was selected with the 19th overall pick of the 1970 NBA Draft by the Cincinnati Royals, more than a few critics were skeptical about how the University of Texas-El Paso star would fare in the NBA. Former Boston Celtics superstar point guard Bob Cousy—now Royals coach and general manager—didn't need convincing, and proudly watched as Archibald outmaneuvered his defenders with his pinpoint passing, outside shooting, and unstoppable drives to the basket. In his third NBA season—the team's first in Kansas City—Archibald led the league in scoring (34 points per game) and assists (11.4), becoming the only player in NBA history to pull off this double-double. Even over 30 years later, no one has duplicated it.

A pioneer for small players everywhere, Tiny Archibald led the league in minutes per game during the 1970–71 season, logging an average of 46 per night.

PLAYERS' RIGHTS

The first collective bargaining agreement between the Players Association and team owners was finalized prior to the 1972–73 season. The terms of the landmark three-year contract included a minimum player salary of $20,000 and a $720 pension for every year of service granted to former players 50 years and older. Larry Fleisher, who would serve more than 25 years as General Counsel, represented the players in the negotiations.

"I had my own style," said Julius Erving. "Call it playground, call it street ball or whatever. It was about pushing at the limits, testing my own imagination."

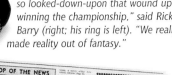

"I don't think there's ever been a team so looked-down-upon that wound up winning the championship," said Rick Barry (right; his ring is left). "We really made reality out of fantasy."

The underdog Warriors proved that regular-season records can be rendered meaningless in the postseason, as newspapers all over San Francisco hailed their victory over the Bullets.

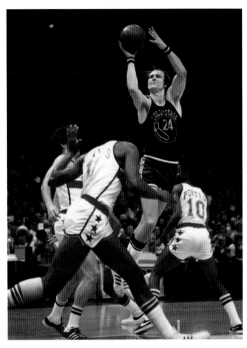

CHAMPIONSHIP TEAMS

1972–73 New York Knicks

1973–74 Boston Celtics

1974–75 Golden State Warriors

A SWEEPING SURPRISE

The Washington Bullets, owners of the best record in the NBA during the 1974–75 season, with 60 wins, defeated the Buffalo Braves in a grueling seven-game series, and the Boston Celtics, last season's champs, in six. Surely the Golden State Warriors, a team the Bullets defeated three out of four times during the season, wouldn't stand in the way of the franchise's first championship. The Bullets had four All-Stars, led by Wes Unseld and Elvin Hayes, while the Warriors primarily featured Rick Barry, the high-scoring, All-Star forward. The odds seemed firmly in the Bullets' favor.

Washington guard Phil Chenier said, "We were confident. Were we overconfident? Maybe that's the case."

The Warriors stole Game 1 of the NBA Finals in Landover, Maryland, 101-95. Due to arena availability, the next two games of the series shifted to Oakland.

"That was a biggie, losing that first game at home and then having to go out there," said Bullets coach K. C. Jones. "That did wonders for Golden State's confidence. It was like going to a beehive."

Thanks to the combination of Barry's sensational scoring and the team's overall depth, the Warriors managed to win the next three games, stunning the Bullets and the NBA.

1975–1977

EPIC BATTLES AND great individual performances marked the mid- to late '70s in the NBA. The first of these memorable moments was the triple-overtime Game 5 classic between the Phoenix Suns and the Boston Celtics in the 1976 NBA Finals. Some called this marathon battle the greatest Finals game of all time after watching a flurry of lead changes and clutch shooting unfold at the storied Boston Garden. Clutch baskets weren't anything new to Bob McAdoo who emerged as one of the greatest shooting big men ever, while the Portland Trail Blazers defeated Philadelphia's band of All-Stars in the 1977 NBA Finals.

Curtis Perry (right) of the Suns was one of the pivotal players in Phoenix's valiant comeback versus the Celtics.

DAVE COWENS: MR. INTENSITY

At 6-9 and 230 pounds, Dave Cowens wasn't the most imposing center ever to play the game, but he may have been the most athletic. What he lacked in size going up against superstars like Wilt Chamberlain and Bob Lanier, he made up for with his selfless team approach and versatile skills. Full-court pressing, pinpoint passing, and diving into crowds for loose balls was all part of his game.

Arriving in Boston before the 1970–71 season, just as the Celtics were coming off their first losing season in 20 years, Cowens averaged 17 points and 15 rebounds, joining veteran John Havlicek in leading Boston's resurgence and earning co-Rookie of the Year honors. The Celtics reclaimed the top spot in the Atlantic Division for the next five campaigns and Cowens, in his third season, earned NBA MVP honors, averaging 20.5 points and 16.2 rebounds. The Celtics won the '74 and '76 NBA Finals, continuing the franchise's rich tradition of championships.

Dave Cowens represented the working class of the NBA, and had an all-out, reckless style of play that earned admiration from teammates and opponents alike.

Celtics win, 128-126—in triple OT

The triple-overtime classic made headlines not only in Boston and Phoenix but throughout the country.

GAME 5 GARDEN CLASSIC

The Boston Celtics were 90 seconds away from a 3-2 NBA Finals series lead over the Phoenix Suns when Sun guard Paul Westphal nailed a fade-away jumper to reduce Boston's lead to 94-91. On the next possession, he tipped the ball away from Boston's Jo Jo White to Sun Alvan Adams, only to be on the receiving end for a layup and the game-tying free throw.

Both teams traded free throws to end regulation, and scored six points apiece before heading into a second overtime. Then John Havlicek nailed a 15-foot shot, seemingly giving the Celtics a 111-110 victory—until referees ruled there was one second left on the clock. The Suns' Gar Heard then hit a 20-footer to send the game into a third overtime. Finally, Boston pulled out the victory, thanks to reserve forward Glenn McDonald who scored six points for the 128-126 triumph.

CHANGING THE GAME

In the mid-1970s, Bill Russell called Bob McAdoo the greatest shooter of all time and, given the roll he embarked on during his first four years in the NBA, few could argue. In his first season with the Buffalo Braves, the 6-9 McAdoo alternated between the center and forward positions and averaged 18 points and

Bob McAdoo (#41) revolutionized the way big men played the game, stretching defenses with his superior perimeter skills as he quickly earned the reputation as one of the best shooting big men of all time.

9.1 rebounds on his way to NBA Rookie of the Year honors. In his second season, McAdoo led the league in shooting percentage with a .547 mark and won the first of three consecutive scoring titles. McAdoo followed that season with what turned out to be his greatest individual campaign ever, as he led the league in scoring (34.5), total points (2,831), total rebounds (1,155), and minutes played (3,539). He also finished fourth in

rebounding (14.1), and fifth in field-goal percentage (.512) and blocked shots per game (2.12). So, it was little surprise that McAdoo earned NBA MVP honors that season. Perhaps most remarkable is that when McAdoo eventually retired following the 1985–86 season, he had not only shot 50 percent or more from the field in seven of his 14 seasons, but had made more than half of his attempts from the perimeter.

CHAMPIONSHIP TEAMS

1975–76 Boston Celtics

1976–77 Portland Trail Blazers

BLAZERMANIA

Billed as the band of All-Stars versus the band of selfless players, the 1977 NBA Finals saw the Philadelphia 76ers go head-to-head against the Portland Trail Blazers.

"The Sixers were like the Who's Who of the NBA," said Lionel Hollins, Portland guard.

"We only had one player who had ever been in the playoffs before," said Portland head coach Jack Ramsay. "I think we were sort of overwhelmed."

The Blazers certainly were, dropping the first two games in Philadelphia, which included a devastating 18-point loss in Game 2 that was marked by a fistfight. Darryl Dawkins, the Sixers' 6-10, 252-pound center, threw a roundhouse punch at Portland's Bobby Gross, only to clock his teammate Doug Collins instead. Maurice Lucas, the Blazers' enforcer, responded with a blow to Dawkins' head.

That turned the series around. Led by Walton, the Blazers blew out the Sixers in Games 3 and 4 by an average of 27 points, and then sealed their first championship by winning Games 5 and 6 as well.

The Blazers featured an All-Star frontline of center Bill Walton (center) and power forward Maurice Lucas, along with a perfect complement of perimeter players: Dave Twardzik (left), Lionel Hollins, Bob Gross, Johnny Davis, Larry Steele, and Herm Gilliam.

1978–1979

THE ABA MAY HAVE FOLDED after the 1975–76 season but its presence was still felt as the '70s drew to a close. Two of the defunct league's biggest stars, George Gervin and David Thompson, made instant impacts in the NBA, showcasing their superb skills and producing one of the most memorable scoring races of all time in the 1977–78 season. The Washington Bullets, who had advanced to the Finals twice before in the decade, finally broke through the championship barrier and defeated the Seattle SuperSonics in a memorable seven-game NBA Finals series in 1978. In the next year's rematch, however, it was Seattle's turn to celebrate.

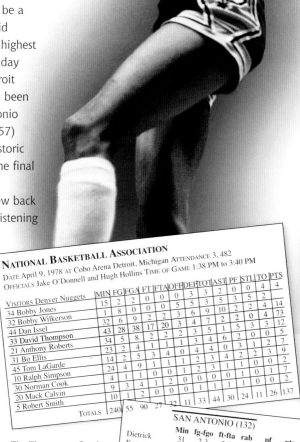

George Gervin rose to the occasion against the New Orleans Jazz, scoring 63 points to win his first scoring title. Gervin finished with a 27.22 average, compared to Thompson's 27.1.

GERVIN VS. THOMPSON: A DUEL TO THE FINISH

The scoring championship appeared to be a lock. The Denver Nuggets' All-Star David Thompson scored 73 points—the third highest point total in NBA history—on the last day of the 1977–78 season against the Detroit Pistons. Thompson, whose average had been trailing George Gervin's of the San Antonio Spurs by a mere fraction (26.78 to 26.57) unfortunately didn't get to enjoy his historic accomplishment for long. Gervin had the final say with a game later that day.

"After I scored the 73 points, we flew back to Denver," said Thompson. "I started listening to the Spurs game. Wilt Chamberlain had set the record for points in one quarter with 31 and it lasted for many years. But my record of 32 points lasted for a few hours, because George scored 33 in the second quarter. By halftime George had scored 53 points. I just turned it off, knowing he would win."

Sure enough he did. Gervin iced the title with 63 points.

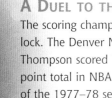

David Thompson dropped 73 points on the Pistons on the last day of the season, only to have his average surpassed by Gervin's 63 later that evening.

The Thompson–Gervin scoring race netted a total of 136 points on the final day of the 1977–78 season.

NATIONAL BASKETBALL ASSOCIATION
DATE April 9, 1978 AT Cobo Arena Detroit, Michigan ATTENDANCE 3,482
OFFICIALS Jake O'Donnell and Hugh Hollins TIME OF GAME 1:38 PM to 3:40 PM

VISITORS Denver Nuggets	MIN	FG	FGA	FT	FTA	OFF	DEF	TOT	AST	PF	STL	TO	PTS
34 Bobby Jones	15	2	2	0	0	0	3	3	2	0	0	4	4
32 Bobby Wilkerson	1	8	0	0	0	5	5	3	5	5	2		
44 Dan Issel	32	6	9	2	2	3	6	9	10	2	2	4	14
33 David Thompson	43	28	38	17	20	2	2	3	4	7	2	2	73
21 Anthony Roberts	34	5	8	2	2	1	3	4	6	2	0	0	12
31 Bo Ellis	23	2	4	1	1	1	3	4	4	2	3	1	5
45 Tom LaGarde	14	2	5	3	4	0	4	4	2	3	1	2	7
10 Ralph Simpson	24	4	9	1	1	1	2	3	4	2	2	3	9
30 Norman Cook	4	1	1	0	0	1	1	0	0	1	0	1	2
20 Mack Calvin	9	3	4	1	2	0	0	1	1	1	1	0	7
5 Robert Smith	10	1	2	0	0	0	1	1	1	1	0	0	2
TOTALS	240	55	90	27	32	11	33	44	30	24	11	26	137

SAN ANTONIO (132)

	Min	fg-fgo	ft-fta	rab	pf	pts
Dietrick	31	2-3	2-2	3	5	6
Kenon	23	6-8	1-2	5	0	13
Poultz	28	3-6	0-0	8	2	6
Gale	13	2-3	0-0	2	2	4
Gervin	33	23-49	17-20	2	3	63
Dampier	12	2-4	0-0	2	1	4
Green	16	0-2	0-0	3	2	0
Olberding	23	3-4	2-2	4	2	8
Bristow	20	3-5	0-0	4	2	6
Silas	20	4-6	2-2	0	2	10
Layton	21	5-8	2-2	0	1	12

BACK-TO-BACK FINALS CLASHES

The 1978 NBA Finals series was a battle between two above-average teams: the 44-38 Washington Bullets versus the 47-35 Seattle SuperSonics. The Bullets had defied critics by upsetting the favored San Antonio Spurs and Philadelphia 76ers en route to the championship games. Meanwhile, the Sonics had recovered from a 5-17 regular-season start (thanks to new head coach Lenny Wilkens) and upset the Portland Trail Blazers in the Western Conference Semifinals.

Game 7 Clincher

Appropriately, the Finals went down to the wire. In Game 7, the Bullets were clinging to a 101-99 lead with 12 seconds remaining, when Wes Unseld was fouled. The 55-percent shooter calmly sank two free throws and helped clinch the franchise's first title in their 17-year history. While it was a game to

Elvin Hayes and Bob Dandridge celebrate the Bullets Game 7 triumph in Seattle of the 1978 Finals.

remember for NBA Finals MVP Unseld, it was a game to forget for Dennis Johnson: the Sonics guard finished 0-14 in Game 7.

Johnson would get his revenge against the Bullets one year later when the teams met again in the Finals. He earned NBA Finals MVP honors in the Sonics' 4-1 series triumph.

Wes Unseld was the rock in Washington's title quest. "Wes was the enforcer who never had to use actual force," said teammate Kevin Grevey.

Dennis Johnson redeemed himself from the 0-14 Game 7 performance in the 1978 NBA Finals and bounced back to claim NBA Finals MVP honors against the Bullets in the '79 series.

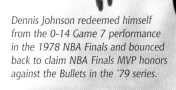

CHAMPIONSHIP TEAMS

1977–78 Washington Bullets

1978–79 Seattle SuperSonics

Individual Honors

1969–70

Scoring Leader:
Jerry West, Los Angeles (31.2)
Rebound Leader:
Elvin Hayes, San Diego (16.9)
Assist Leader:
Lenny Wilkens, Seattle (9.1)
Free-Throw Leader:
Flynn Robinson, Milwaukee (.898)
MVP: Willis Reed, New York
Rookie of the Year:
Kareem Abdul-Jabbar, Milwaukee
Coach of the Year:
Red Holzman, New York
NBA Finals MVP:
Willis Reed, New York
Hall of Fame Class:
Bernard L. Carnevale, Coach
Robert E. Davies, Player

1970–71

Scoring Leader:
Kareem Abdul-Jabbar,
Milwaukee (31.7)
Rebound Leader:
Wilt Chamberlain,
Los Angeles (18.2)
Assist Leader:
Norm Van Lier, Cincinnati (10.2)
Free-Throw Leader:
Chet Walker, Chicago (.859)
MVP: Kareem Abdul-Jabbar,
Milwaukee
Rookies of the Year:
Dave Cowens, Boston and
Geoff Petrie, Portland
Coach of the Year:
Dick Motta, Chicago
NBA Finals MVP:
Kareem Abdul-Jabbar, Milwaukee
Hall of Fame Class:
Robert J. Cousy, Player
Robert L. Pettit, Player
Abraham Saperstein, Contributor

1971–72

Scoring Leader:
Kareem Abdul-Jabbar,
Milwaukee (34.8)
Rebound Leader:
Wilt Chamberlain,
Los Angeles (19.2)
Assist Leader:
Jerry West, Los Angeles (9.7)
Free-Throw Leader:
Jack Marin, Baltimore (.894)
MVP: Kareem Abdul-Jabbar,
Milwaukee
Rookie of the Year:
Sidney Wicks, Portland
Coach of the Year:
Bill Sharman, Los Angeles
NBA Finals MVP:
Wilt Chamberlain, Los Angeles
Hall of Fame Class:
Edgar A. Diddle, Coach
Robert L. Douglas, Contributor
Paul Endacott, Player
Max Friedman, Player
Edward Gottlieb, Contributor
W. R. Clifford Wells, Contributor

1972–73

Scoring Leader:
Nate Archibald,
Kansas City/Omaha (34.0)
Rebound Leader:
Wilt Chamberlain,
Los Angeles (18.6)
Assist Leader:
Nate Archibald,
Kansas City/Omaha (11.4)
Free-Throw Leader:
Rick Barry, Golden State (.902)
MVP: Dave Cowens, Boston
Rookie of the Year:
Bob McAdoo, Buffalo

Coach of the Year:
Tom Heinsohn, Boston
NBA Finals MVP:
Willis Reed, New York
Hall of Fame Class:
John Beckman, Player
Bruce Drake, Coach
Arthur C. Lonborg, Coach
Elmer H. Ripley, Contributor
Adolph Schayes, Player
John R. Wooden, Coach

1973–74

Scoring Leader:
Bob McAdoo, Buffalo (30.6)
Rebound Leader:
Elvin Hayes, Capital Bullets (18.1)
Assist Leader:
Ernie DiGregorio, Buffalo (8.2)
Free-Throw Leader:
Ernie DiGregorio, Buffalo (.902)
Steal Leader:
Larry Steele, Portland (2.68)
Blocked-Shot Leader:
Elmore Smith, Los Angeles (4.85)
MVP: Kareem Abdul-Jabbar,
Milwaukee
Rookie of the Year:
Ernie DiGregorio, Buffalo
Coach of the Year:
Ray Scott, Detroit
NBA Finals MVP:
John Havlicek, Boston
Hall of Fame Class:
Harry A. Fisher, Contributor
Maurice Podoloff, Contributor
Ernest J. Schmidt, Player

1974–75

Scoring Leader:
Bob McAdoo, Buffalo (34.5)
Rebound Leader:
Wes Unseld, Washington (14.8)
Assist Leader:
Kevin Porter, Washington (8.0)

Free-Throw Leader:
Rick Barry, Golden State (.904)
Steal Leader:
Rick Barry, Golden State (2.85)
Blocked-Shot Leader:
Kareem Abdul-Jabbar,
Milwaukee (3.26)
MVP: Bob McAdoo, Buffalo
Rookie of the Year:
Keith Wilkes, Golden State
Coach of the Year:
Phil Johnson, Kansas City/Omaha
NBA Finals MVP:
Rick Barry, Golden State
Hall of Fame Class:
Joseph R. Brennan, Player
Emil S. Liston, Contributor
William F. Russell, Player
Robert P. Vandivier, Player

1975–76

Scoring Leader:
Bob McAdoo, Buffalo (31.1)
Rebound Leader:
Kareem Abdul-Jabbar,
Los Angeles (16.9)
Assist Leader:
Donald Watts, Seattle (8.1)
Free-Throw Leader:
Rick Barry, Golden State (.923)
Steal Leader:
Donald Watts, Seattle (3.18)
Blocked-Shot Leader:
Kareem Abdul-Jabbar,
Los Angeles (4.12)
MVP: Kareem Abdul-Jabbar,
Los Angeles
Rookie of the Year:
Alvan Adams, Phoenix
Coach of the Year:
Bill Fitch, Cleveland
NBA Finals MVP:
Jo Jo White, Boston

Hall of Fame Class:
Thomas J. Gola, Player
Edward W. Krause, Player
Harry Litwack, Coach
William W. Sharman, Player

1976–77

Scoring Leader:
Pete Maravich, New Orleans (31.1)
Rebound Leader:
Bill Walton, Portland (14.4)
Assist Leader:
Don Buse, Indiana (8.5)
Free-Throw Leader:
Ernie DiGregorio, Buffalo (.945)
Steal Leader:
Don Buse, Indiana (3.47)
Blocked-Shot Leader:
Bill Walton, Portland (3.25)
MVP: Kareem Abdul-Jabbar,
Los Angeles
**Rookie of
the Year:**
Adrian Dantley,
Buffalo
**Coach of
the Year:**
Tom Nissalke,
Houston
NBA Finals MVP:
Bill Walton, Portland

Hall of Fame Class:
Elgin Baylor, Player
Charles T. Cooper, Player
Lauren Gale, Player
William C. Johnson, Player
Frank J. McGuire, Coach

1977–78

Scoring Leader:
George Gervin, San Antonio (27.2)
Rebound Leader:
Truck Robinson,
New Orleans (15.7)
Assist Leader:
Kevin Porter,
Detroit/New Jersey (10.2)
Free-Throw Leader:
Rick Barry, Golden State (.924)

Steal Leader:
Ron Lee, Phoenix (2.74)
Blocked-Shot Leader:
George Johnson, New Jersey (3.38)
MVP: Bill Walton, Portland
Rookie of the Year:
Walter Davis, Phoenix
Coach of the Year:
Hubie Brown, Atlanta
NBA Finals MVP:
Wes Unseld, Washington
Hall of Fame Class:
Paul J. Arizin, Player
Joseph F. Fulks, Player
Clifford O. Hagan, Player
John P. Nucatola, Referee
James C. Pollard, Player

1978–79

Scoring Leader:
George Gervin, San Antonio (29.6)
Rebound Leader:
Moses Malone, Houston (17.6)
Assist Leader:
Kevin Porter, Detroit (13.4)
Free-Throw Leader:
Rick Barry, Houston (.947)
Steal Leader:
M. L. Carr, Detroit (2.46)
Blocked-Shot Leader:
Kareem Abdul-Jabbar,
Los Angeles (3.95)
MVP: Moses Malone, Houston
Rookie of the Year:
Phil Ford, Kansas City
Coach of the Year:
Cotton Fitzsimmons, Kansas City
NBA Finals MVP:
Dennis Johnson, Seattle
Hall of Fame Class:
Justin M. (Sam) Barry, Coach
Wilton N. Chamberlain, Player
James E. Enright, Referee
Edgar S. Hickey, Coach
John B. McLendon, Jr., Coach
Raymond J. Meyer, Coach
Peter F. Newell, Coach

1980–1983

THE 1979–80 SEASON ushered in a new era of basketball greatness, featuring two rookies starring on opposite ends of the coast: Magic Johnson in Los Angeles and Larry Bird in Boston. Rivals ever since the 1979 NCAA championship game where they clashed leading their respective schools, both players soon became the talk of the league.

The early '80s also featured one of the greatest teams in NBA history: the 1983 Philadelphia 76ers. Led by Moses Malone and Julius Erving, the Sixers posted a 65-17 regular-season record and swept the Lakers in the NBA Finals.

AMERICA'S FAVORITE RIVALS

Larry Bird's greatness was immediately evident during his rookie season, when he led Boston to a 32-game improvement over the previous season. The Celtics' leap from last to first place in the Atlantic Division standings helped edge Bird past Magic Johnson in the 1980 NBA Rookie of the Year voting. Johnson, the 20-year-old rookie point guard, helped lead the Lakers to 60 regular-season wins and the 1980 NBA title. Although the teams wouldn't meet in the NBA Finals until 1984, it was clear that their rivalry was blossoming—as was the league's popularity.

Excellent shooting was only a part of Bird's all-around game.

A stunned Magic Johnson (center) and his teammates celebrate the 1980 NBA title.

Larry Bird and Magic Johnson graced the cover of the 1980–81 NBA Guide in only their second seasons, showing how important their rivalry was to the game.

Even Magic Johnson (left) and Kareem Abdul-Jabbar (right) couldn't stop Moses Malone (center) and the 76ers in the 1982–83 season.

MOSES AND THE 1983 76ERS

Philadelphia 76ers fans were frustrated. Since the franchise's last championship in 1967, the team had reached the NBA Finals three times (1977, '80, '82), only to leave broken-hearted every time. Though the Sixers featured All-Star high-flyer Julius Erving along with Maurice Cheeks, Andrew Toney, and Bobby Jones, the championship somehow eluded them. But not for long. The Sixers acquired two-time NBA MVP Moses Malone prior to the '82–83 season and the team became a dominant force.

How important was the arrival of Malone? The Sixers, who had finished 20th in rebounding the prior season, now finished first. Malone averaged 24.5 points and led the league in rebounding with 15.3 boards per game while picking up his third MVP award. The team finished with a 65–17 record and when asked how the Sixers would fare in the playoffs, Malone predicted a four-game sweep in each series with his famous quote, "Fo'. Fo'. Fo'." He was close. The 76ers went 12–1 and swept the Lakers in the NBA Finals.

PAT RILEY'S DEBUT

Before he led the Lakers to four NBA titles in the 1980s as a head coach, Pat Riley (left) served as an assistant coach on the Los Angeles bench during the 1979–80 season. Riley replaced former head coach Paul Westhead (right) only 11 games into the 1981–82 season.

CHAMPIONSHIP TEAMS

1979–80 Los Angeles Lakers

1980–81 Boston Celtics

1981–82 Los Angeles Lakers

1982–83 Philadelphia 76ers

1984–1985

SCORING—THERE WAS PLENTY of it in the early to mid-80s. The once untouchable records appeared to now be falling on a yearly basis. The Detroit Pistons visited the Denver Nuggets for a regular-season game and produced mile-high results. Both teams combined to score 370 points as the Pistons squeaked by with a 186-184 win, establishing six records in the process, including most field goals made by two teams (142). Individual scoring also took center stage during this period as Bernard King showed why he was one of the NBA's greatest individual scorers and Kareem Abdul-Jabbar eclipsed Wilt Chamberlain as the NBA's all-time scoring champion.

Fan
Amazin'
to score

One of the most beloved players ever to wear a Knick uniform, Bernard King's feat was big news in New York.

THE HIGHEST SCORING GAME IN NBA HISTORY

This regular-season game set the standard for offensive excess. When the Detroit Pistons visited the Denver Nuggets on December 13, 1983, it took three hours and eleven minutes for the teams to shatter six NBA records as part of the highest scoring game in NBA history—186-184. The record-breaking night included such milestones as: most points by two teams (370), most points by one team (Detroit, 186), most players with 40 or more points (4), most field goals made by two teams (142), most field goals made by one team (Detroit, 74), and most assists by both teams (93).

The 9,655 fans lucky enough to be in attendance at McNichols Arena on that frosty night saw the Pistons and Nuggets each run up halftime scores of 74. By the end of the third quarter, the Nuggets led 113-108.

The triple-overtime classic produced numerous lead changes and missed opportunities for each team to seal the victory. When the Pistons seized the lead for good with less than two minutes remaining in the third overtime, it was, ironically, Detroit's defense that saved the day as they held Denver in check.

"At the end of the game," said Alex English, who tied Detroit's Isiah Thomas as the game's second-highest scorer with 47 points, "I just remembered being bone-tired."

Kiki Vandeweghe shined the brightest in the highest scoring game, leading all scorers with 51 points. The Nuggets forward converted on 21 of 29 field goals and 9 of 11 free throws.

	1	2	3	4	1OT	2OT	3OT	Tot
Detroit	38	36	34	37	14	12	15	186
Denver	34	40	39	32	14	12	13	184

Pistons win a 'nuke-out'

Did you know that the highest scoring game in NBA history only produced two three-point field goals? One by each team.

Isiah Thomas led the Pistons with 47 points on 18 for 34 shooting, and also contributed a game-high 17 assists in Detroit's 186-184 triple-overtime victory in Denver.

stic 50's
st in 17 years
straight games

By Kevin Kernan

DALLAS — Bernard King was Superman again last night.

In a breathless, 41-minute encore performance, King rewrote the Knick record book *again*, scoring 50 points for the second straight night and single-handedly leading the Knicks to a dramatic 105-98 victory over the Mavericks.

No one had scored 50 points in two straight NBA games since Rick Barry, then with San Francisco, had 50 against the Celtics Feb. 14, 1967 and 52 against Cincinnati two nights later. No one had scored 50 on successive nights since Wilt Chamberlain hit 52 against Cincinnati and then Detroit Feb. 17-18, 1964.

Bernard will attempt to become the only player other than Chamberlain to hit 50 in three straight games when the Knicks play in Houston Saturday.

King's fandango of fury left 14,209 fans silent, Mark Aguirre stunned, Hubie Brown nearly speechless and King's

teammates exhausted and enthralled, sharing in his glorious triumph.

The truth is, they may have wanted it more than King.

With the game clock down to nine seconds and King perched at 48 points, the entire Knick bench was standing and screaming, "Give it to Bernard. Do it B."

Brown was 15 feet up the sideline leading the chants of his oversized cheerleaders.

Rory Sparrow, who had glanced at the scoreboard and knew King had 48 points, waited until King broke toward him to give him the ball.

"If I didn't give it to him, my teammates would have killed me,"

... and sets up offense in last night's 105-98 Knick victory over Mavericks.

Continued on Page 66

SCORING KING

A Texas Tornado swept across San Antonio and Dallas causing insurmountable damage to the Spurs and Mavericks during the 1984–85 season. In a 48-hour period, Bernard King of the New York Knicks tallied 100 points with back-to-back 50-point games. On January 31 and February 1, King converted 40 of 58 field-goal attempts (77 percent) and 20 of 22 from the free-throw line. The 50-point specials arrived not too long after the Knicks' small forward set a team record on Christmas Day, when he dropped 60 against the New Jersey Nets. King went on to lead the league in scoring that season with a 32.9 mark.

The unstoppable sky-hook served Kareem Abdul-Jabbar extremely well during his Hall of Fame career.

KAREEM SKY-HOOKS TO SCORING GREATNESS

An unlikely location for one of basketball's greatest records, Las Vegas, Nevada, was the part-time home to the Utah Jazz during the 1983–84 season. When the Lakers visited the Jazz on April 5, 1984, Kareem Abdul-Jabbar was on the cusp of surpassing the greatest scoring force the game has ever seen—Wilt Chamberlain. The Big Dipper had amassed 31,419 points in 14 seasons. Now it was Abdul-Jabbar's turn to rewrite the record book, and to no one's surprise, he would use his patented sky-hook, one of basketball's greatest offensive weapons, to put himself over the top. With a little more than 6 minutes remaining in the fourth quarter, Abdul-Jabbar received a pass from teammate Magic Johnson and immediately went to work on 7-4 Jazz center, Mark Eaton. Abdul-Jabbar released a 10-foot sky-hook that swished beautifully to the roar of the sold-out crowd for the all-time NBA scoring record.

Abdul-Jabbar scored an additional 6,967 points over the course of the next five seasons before retiring following the 1988–89 season with 38,387 points.

The ball used to score the historic basket is proudly displayed at the Naismith Memorial Basketball Hall of Fame in Springfield, Massachusetts.

IN GAME APRIL 5, 1984 LAS VEGAS, NEV. K. ABDUL JABBAR SCORED 31,421st POINT (NBA SCORING RECORD)

SPALDING

CHAMPIONSHIP TEAMS

1983–84 Boston Celtics

1984–85 Los Angeles Lakers

SILENCING THE DEMONS

The Lakers needed a championship. After losing a heartbreaking seven-game series to the Boston Celtics in the 1984 NBA Finals, the Lakers would earn another shot against their bitter rivals—their ninth head-to-head championship battle—and this time the outcome would be different. After getting pounded by 34 points in Game 1 ("The Memorial Day Massacre"), 38-year-old Kareem Abdul-Jabbar led the Lakers to the Game 6 clincher on the parquet.

Pat Riley (top at right) and the Los Angeles Lakers did something no other franchise could do: win a title in Boston Garden.

1986–1987

THE BOSTON CELTICS and the Los Angeles Lakers continued to dominate during the '80s. The '86 Celtics enjoyed one of the greatest seasons ever as they rolled to a 49-1 regular season and a playoff home record, while the Lakers continued to stockpile the championships. Memorable moves and games ran rampant during this period, whether it was Magic Johnson confounding the Celtics with his "junior-junior" sky-hook or Larry Bird stealing the Eastern Finals from the Pistons. Yet the Celtics and Lakers didn't hog all the headlines—Michael Jordan continued to amaze as he set a single-game playoff record against the Boston Celtics in the 1986 NBA Playoffs.

Bill Walton earned NBA Sixth Man of the Year honors and helped propel Boston to the 1986 title.

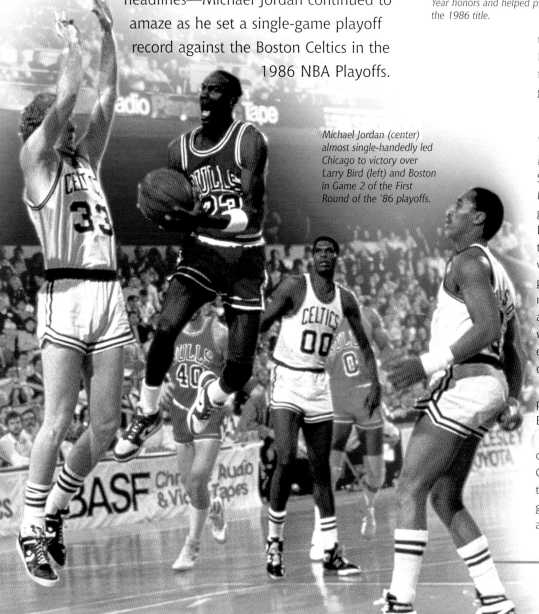

Michael Jordan (center) almost single-handedly led Chicago to victory over Larry Bird (left) and Boston in Game 2 of the First Round of the '86 playoffs.

TEAM FOR THE AGES

The 1985–86 Boston Celtics certainly make a strong case for being the greatest team ever. Boasting one of the greatest frontlines in NBA history—Larry Bird, Kevin McHale, and Robert Parish—plus a healthy Bill Walton off the bench, the Celtics posted a 40-1 record at Boston Garden en route to the best mark in franchise history: 63-19. Boston rolled through the first three rounds of the 1986 NBA playoffs, losing only one game before facing the Houston Rockets in the Finals. Led by Bird, Boston sealed the title in six games as the 6-9 forward achieved a triple-double in the final game of the championship series.

"GOD DISGUISED AS MICHAEL JORDAN"

Strongly encouraged to sit out the playoffs, Michael Jordan had missed 64 regular-season games after breaking a bone in his foot. The Bulls organization cringed at the thought of the rising superstar jeopardizing his career, while Jordan cringed at the thought of not playing. In Game 2 of the 1986 First Round matchup against the Boston Celtics, Jordan assured the organization and everyone who was watching that he had fully recovered. He ended up setting a playoff record with a jaw-dropping, 63-point display in Boston Garden.

Unfortunately for Chicago fans, Jordan's point explosion wasn't enough to keep the Bulls from losing 135-131 in double-overtime.

"I didn't think anyone was capable of doing what Michael has done to us," said Celtics superstar forward Larry Bird. "He is the most exciting, awesome player in the game today. I think it's just God disguised as Michael Jordan."

*gic stole a page out of
nmate Kareem Abdul-
bar's offensive playbook
en he sky-hooked the
ers to a crucial Game 3
ory over the Celtics.*

MAGIC'S JUNIOR-JUNIOR SKY-HOOK

Game 4 of the 1987 NBA Finals was a close one. After Kareem Abdul-Jabbar missed the second of his back-to-back free throws there at Boston Garden, Celtic Kevin McHale got the ball but was pushed by Mychal Thompson of the Lakers. The ball then went out of bounds and was rewarded to the Lakers. Trailing 106-105, Los Angeles had one last chance, and that's all that Magic Johnson needed.

The Lakers superstar received the inbounds pass to the left of the key and briefly flirted with the idea of shooting a 20-footer, but McHale's defense made him reconsider. Johnson then maneuvered into the key, where he was greeted by a sea of arms as McHale, Larry Bird, and Robert Parish all converged on the superstar. Undeterred, Magic lofted a sky-hook just over Parish's fingertips which hit net, much to the dismay of Celtics coach K. C. Jones, who was watching from the bench a few feet away.

"You expect to lose on a sky-hook," said Bird after the game. "You don't expect it to be from Magic."

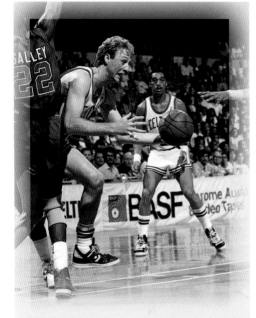

MAN OF STEAL

The goal for Detroit was simple: inbound the ball and go home with a 3-2 series lead in the Eastern Conference Finals against the defending-champion Boston Celtics. With five seconds left and the Pistons clinging to a 107-106 lead, Isiah Thomas tossed the ball to teammate Bill Laimbeer. Larry Bird immediately left his man, swooped in, stole the ball, and somehow kept balance on one foot as he hit a streaking Dennis Johnson for the game-winning layup: Boston 108, Detroit 107.

CHAMPIONSHIP TEAMS

1985–86 Boston Celtics

1986–87 Los Angeles Lakers

1988–1989

THE '80S CLOSED OUT IN dramatic fashion, similar to the way they began. The Lakers continued winning championships, sealing their status as the team of the decade with five titles in ten years. While the Lakers enjoyed their view from the NBA's mountaintop, new teams were threatening, most notably the Detroit Pistons, who advanced to back-to-back Finals. Without a lot of fanfare, Alex English of the Denver Nuggets was scoring at a record pace while Michael Jordan continued to break opponents' hearts.

Pat Riley (left) proved to be the master motivator in placing pressure on his team to repeat as NBA champions, which they did, thanks to James Worthy's MVP performance.

THE RILEY CHAMPIONSHIP GUARANTEE

How did the Lakers celebrate their 1987 NBA championship, their fourth of the decade? They didn't. One day after defeating the Boston Celtics in a hard-fought six-game series, Pat Riley, the Lakers head coach, issued this proclamation: the Lakers will win the title next year—guaranteed. Instead of kicking back and enjoying their championship success, the players were haunted during the offseason by Riley's words. After all, no team had won back-to-back titles since the Celtics in 1968 and 1969.

The Lakers responded to Riley's challenge by posting the league's best record of 62-20 and advancing to the NBA Finals. Four victories then separated the Lakers from true greatness. The Detroit Pistons had L.A. on the ropes, up 3-2, but the Lakers bounced back, winning Game 6 at home and then sealing their place in history by way of James Worthy's triple-double performance in Game 7.

CHAMPIONSHIP TEAMS

1987–88 Los Angeles Lakers

1988–89 Detroit Pistons

MILE-HIGH NUMBERS

While players such as Julius Erving, Magic Johnson, Larry Bird, and Michael Jordan were garnering the most headlines, Alex English was quietly going about his business as one of the greatest scorers of all time. The 6-7 small forward led the league in scoring during the '80s with 19,682 points, and was the first player in NBA history to score 2,000 or more points for eight straight seasons. Selected with the 23rd overall pick in the 1976 NBA Draft by the Milwaukee Bucks, English joined Denver in his fourth season and enjoyed a 10-year career in which he set 31 Nuggets' records, including points scored (21,645), scoring average (25.9), most points and highest scoring average in a season (2,414 and 29.8 in 1985–86), assists (3,679), games played (837), and minutes played (29,893).

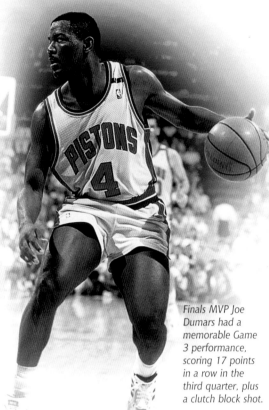

Finals MVP Joe Dumars had a memorable Game 3 performance, scoring 17 points in a row in the third quarter, plus a clutch block shot.

THE SHOT

In a career filled with defining moments, this may be one of Michael Jordan's personal favorites. During Game 5 of the First Round of the 1989 NBA Playoffs, the Cleveland Cavaliers—owners of a franchise-best 57-25 record—took on a young Bulls team that had been unsuccessful in their six regular-season meetings against their Central Division rival. However, with three seconds remaining in this pivotal game, and the Cavs clinging to a 100-99 point lead, records were rendered meaningless. All that mattered was this final possession and, with the game on the line, Jordan delivered. The 6-6 shooting guard rose to the occasion, suspended in midair, waiting for his defender Craig Ehlo to pass as he lofted a jumper that hit nothing but net. Bulls 101, Cavs 100.

Michael Jordan on The Shot: "That's probably the biggest shot I've had in the NBA, mainly because I had put my credibility on the line. I had said we could beat this team."

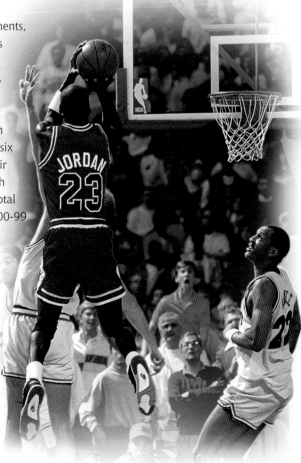

MOTORING TO A CHAMPIONSHIP

The Detroit Pistons' championship climb seemed to always come so close before being thwarted in heartbreaking fashion. In the 1987 Eastern Conference Finals, their rivals, the Boston Celtics, shattered their hopes in a thrilling seven-game series. The following year, it was the Los Angeles Lakers' turn, as they rebounded from a 3-2 Finals deficit to defeat the Pistons in seven games.

The 1988–89 season would be different. One of the greatest defensive teams of the modern era, the Pistons limited their opponents to 100.8 points per game and a field-goal percentage of .447, ranking second in the NBA in both categories. The Pistons posted the NBA's best record at 63-19 and simply would not be denied, compiling an 11-2 mark en route to another Finals appearance against the Lakers.

Los Angeles suffered a pair of key injuries in that series (Byron Scott and Magic Johnson) but Detroit didn't show any compassion, sweeping the Lakers and securing the franchise's first championship, while earning Joe Dumars MVP honors along the way.

Individual Honors

1979–80

Scoring Leader:
George Gervin, San Antonio (33.1)
Rebound Leader:
Swen Nater, San Diego (15.0)
Assist Leader:
Micheal Ray Richardson,
New York (10.2)
Free-Throw Percentage Leader:
Rick Barry, Houston (.935)
Steal Leader:
Micheal Ray Richardson,
New York (3.23)
Blocked-Shot Leader:
Kareem Abdul-Jabbar,
Los Angeles (3.41)
Three-Point Percentage Leader:
Fred Brown, Seattle (.443)
MVP: Kareem Abdul-Jabbar,
Los Angeles
Rookie of the Year:
Larry Bird, Boston
Coach of the Year:
Bill Fitch, Boston
NBA Finals MVP:
Magic Johnson, Los Angeles
Hall of Fame Class:
Lester Harrison, Contributor
Jerry R. Lucas, Player
Oscar P. Robertson, Player
Everett F. Shelton, Coach
J. Dallas Shirley, Referee
Jerry A. West, Player

1980–81

Scoring Leader:
Adrian Dantley, Utah (30.7)
Rebound Leader:
Moses Malone, Houston (14.8)
Assist Leader:
Kevin Porter, Washington (9.1)
Free-Throw Percentage Leader:
Calvin Murphy, Houston (.958)
Steal Leader:
Magic Johnson, Los Angeles (3.43)

Blocked-Shot Leader:
George Johnson, San Antonio (3.39)
Three-Point Percentage Leader:
Brian Taylor, San Diego (.383)
MVP: Julius Erving, Philadelphia
Rookie of the Year:
Darrell Griffith, Utah
Coach of the Year:
Jack McKinney, Indiana
NBA Finals MVP:
Cedric Maxwell, Boston
Hall of Fame Class:
Thomas B. Barlow, Player
Ferenc Hepp, Contributor
J. Walter Kennedy, Contributor
Arad A. McCutchan, Coach

1981–82

Scoring Leader:
George Gervin, San Antonio (32.3)
Rebound Leader:
Moses Malone, Houston (14.7)
Assist Leader:
Johnny Moore, San Antonio (9.7)
Free-Throw Percentage Leader:
Kyle Macy, Phoenix (.899)
Steal Leader:
Magic Johnson, Los Angeles (2.67)
Blocked-Shot Leader:
George Johnson, San Antonio (3.12)
Three-Point Percentage Leader:
Campy Russell, New York (.439)
MVP: Moses Malone, Houston
Rookie of the Year:
Buck Williams, New Jersey
Coach of the Year:
Gene Shue, Washington
NBA Finals MVP:
Magic Johnson, Los Angeles
Hall of Fame Class:
Everett N. Case, Coach
Alva O. Duer, Contributor
Clarence E. Gaines, Coach
Harold E. Greer, Player
Slater N. Martin, Player

Frank V. Ramsey, Jr., Player
Willis Reed, Jr., Player

1982–83

Scoring Leader:
Alex English, Denver (28.4)
Rebound Leader:
Moses Malone, Philadelphia (15.3)
Assist Leader:
Magic Johnson, Los Angeles (10.5)
Free-Throw Percentage Leader:
Calvin Murphy, Houston (.920)
Steal Leader:
Micheal Ray Richardson,
Golden State/New Jersey (2.84)
Blocked-Shot Leader:
Tree Rollins, Atlanta (4.29)
Three-Point Percentage Leader:
Mike Dunleavy, San Antonio (.345)
MVP: Moses Malone, Philadelphia
Rookie of the Year:
Terry Cummings, San Diego
Coach of the Year:
Don Nelson, Milwaukee
NBA Finals MVP:
Moses Malone, Philadelphia
Defensive Player of the Year:
Sidney Moncrief, Milwaukee
Sixth Man Award:
Bobby Jones, Philadelphia
Hall of Fame Class:
William W. Bradley, Player
David A. DeBusschere, Player
Lloyd R. Leith, Referee
Dean E. Smith, Coach
John (Jack) K. Twyman, Player
Louis G. Wilke, Contributor

1983–84

Scoring Leader:
Adrian Dantley, Utah (30.6)
Rebound Leader:
Moses Malone, Philadelphia (13.4)
Assist Leader:
Magic Johnson, Los Angeles (13.1)

Free-Throw Percentage Leader:
Larry Bird, Boston (.888)
Steal Leader:
Rickey Green, Utah (2.65)
Blocked-Shot Leader:
Mark Eaton, Utah (4.28)
Three-Point Percentage Leader:
Darrell Griffith, Utah (.361)
MVP: Larry Bird, Boston
Rookie of the Year:
Ralph Sampson, Houston
Coach of the Year:
Frank Layden, Utah
NBA Finals MVP:
Larry Bird, Boston
Defensive Player of the Year:
Sidney Moncrief, Milwaukee
Sixth Man Award:
Kevin McHale, Boston
Hall of Fame Class:
Clifford B. Fagan, Contributor
James H. (Jack) Gardner, Coach
John Havlicek, Player
Samuel (Sam) Jones, Player
Edward S. Steitz, Contributor

1984–85

Scoring Leader:
Bernard King, New York (32.9)
Rebound Leader:
Moses Malone, Philadelphia (13.1)
Assist Leader:
Isiah Thomas, Detroit (13.9)
Free-Throw Percentage Leader:
Kyle Macy, Phoenix (.907)
Steal Leader:
Micheal Ray Richardson,
New Jersey (2.96)
Blocked-Shot Leader:
Mark Eaton, Utah (5.56)
Three-Point Percentage Leader:
Byron Scott, Los Angeles Lakers
MVP: Larry Bird, Boston
Rookie of the Year:
Michael Jordan, Chicago

Coach of the Year:
Don Nelson, Milwaukee
NBA Finals MVP:
Kareem Abdul-Jabbar,
Los Angeles Lakers
Defensive Player of the Year:
Mark Eaton, Utah
Sixth Man Award:
Kevin McHale, Boston
Hall of Fame Class:
Senda Berenson Abbott,
Contributor
W. Harold Anderson, Coach
Alfred N. Cervi, Player
Marv K. Harshman, Coach
Bertha F. Teague, Contributor
Nate Thurmond, Player
L. Margaret Wade, Coach

1985–86

Scoring Leader:
Dominique Wilkins, Atlanta (30.3)
Rebound Leader:
Bill Laimbeer, Detroit (13.1)
Assist Leader:
Magic Johnson,
Los Angeles Lakers (12.6)
Free-Throw Percentage Leaders:
Larry Bird, Boston and
Chris Mullin, Golden State (.896)
Steal Leader:
Alvin Robertson,
San Antonio (3.67)
Blocked-Shot Leader:
Manute Bol, Washington (4.96)
Three-Point Pctg. Leaders:
Craig Hodges, Milwaukee and
Trent Tucker, New York (.451)
MVP: Larry Bird, Boston
Rookie of the Year:
Patrick Ewing, New York
Coach of the Year:
Mike Fratello, Atlanta
NBA Finals MVP:
Larry Bird, Boston
Defensive Player of the Year:
Alvin Robertson, San Antonio
Sixth Man Award:
Bill Walton, Boston

Most Improved Player:
Alvin Robertson, San Antonio
Hall of Fame Class:
William J. Cunningham, Player
Thomas W. Heinsohn, Player
William "Red" Holzman, Coach
Zigmund "Red" Mihalik, Referee
Fred R. Taylor, Coach
Stanley H. Watts, Coach

1986–87

Scoring Leader:
Michael Jordan, Chicago (37.1)
Rebound Leader:
Charles Barkley, Philadelphia (14.6)
Assist Leader:
Magic Johnson,
Los Angeles Lakers (12.2)
Free-Throw Percentage Leader:
Larry Bird, Boston (.910)
Steal Leader:
Alvin Robertson, San Antonio (3.21)
Blocked-Shot Leader:
Mark Eaton, Utah (4.06)
Three-Point Percentage Leader:
Kiki Vandeweghe, Portland (.481)
MVP: Magic Johnson,
Los Angeles Lakers
Rookie of the Year:
Chuck Person, Indiana
Coach of the Year:
Mike Schuler, Portland
NBA Finals MVP:
Magic Johnson, Los Angeles Lakers
Defensive Player of the Year:
Michael Cooper, Los Angeles Lakers
Sixth Man Award:
Ricky Pierce, Milwaukee
Most Improved Player:
Dale Ellis, Seattle
Hall of Fame Class:
Richard F. Barry, Player
Walter Frazier, Player
Robert J. Houbregs, Player
Peter P. Maravich, Player
Robert Wanzer, Player

1987–88

Scoring Leader:
Michael Jordan, Chicago (35.0)
Rebound Leader:
Michael Cage, Los Angeles
Clippers (13.03)
Assist Leader:
John Stockton, Utah (13.8)
Free-Throw Percentage Leader:
Jack Sikma, Milwaukee (.922)
Steal Leader:
Michael Jordan, Chicago (3.16)
Blocked-Shot Leader:
Mark Eaton, Utah (3.71)
Three-Point Percentage Leader:
Craig Hodges, Milwaukee/Phoenix
MVP: Michael Jordan, Chicago
Rookie of the Year:
Mark Jackson, New York
Coach of the Year:
Doug Moe, Denver
NBA Finals MVP:
James Worthy, Los Angeles Lakers
Defensive Player of the Year:
Michael Jordan, Chicago
Sixth Man Award:
Roy Tarpley, Dallas
Most Improved Player:
Kevin Duckworth, Portland
Hall of Fame Class:
Clyde E. Lovellette, Player
Robert McDermott, Player
Ralph H. Miller, Coach
Westley S. Unseld, Player

1988–89

Scoring Leader:
Michael Jordan, Chicago (32.5)
Rebound Leader:
Hakeem Olajuwon, Houston (13.5)
Assist Leader:
John Stockton, Utah (13.6)
Free-Throw Percentage Leader:
Magic Johnson,
Los Angeles Lakers (.911)
Steal Leader:
John Stockton, Utah (3.21)
Blocked-Shot Leader:
Manute Bol, Golden State (4.31)

Three-Point Percentage Leader:
Jon Sundvold, Miami (.522)
MVP: Magic Johnson,
Los Angeles Lakers
Rookie of the Year:
Mitch Richmond, Golden State
Coach of the Year:
Cotton Fitzsimmons, Phoenix
NBA Finals MVP:
Joe Dumars, Detroit
Defensive Player of the Year:
Mark Eaton, Utah
Sixth Man Award:
Eddie Johnson, Phoenix
Most Improved Player:
Kevin Johnson, Phoenix
Hall of Fame Class:
William "Pop" Gates, Player
K. C. Jones, Player
Leonard (Lenny) Wilkens, Player

1990–1993

A NEW ERA WAS BECKONING. As the 1980s drew to a close, so did the championship brilliance of two of its mightiest heavyweights, the Los Angeles Lakers and Boston Celtics. The new guard had arrived and it was flexing its considerable muscle. The Detroit Pistons picked up where they left off at the end of the decade by winning the first NBA title of the '90s and further cementing their place among the NBA's all-time great teams. Looming in the background, however, were the Chicago Bulls, their Central Division nemesis, who after three consecutive playoff losses to Detroit, finally broke through and embarked on one of the greatest championship runs in NBA history.

The championship wait was finally over. After seven long years, Michael Jordan realized his dream of winning an NBA title when the Chicago Bulls defeated the Los Angeles Lakers in five games in the 1991 NBA Finals.

A Bull Run

While no one ever questioned Michael Jordan's individual athletic talents, many wondered if he shared the ability of Bird, Magic, and Isiah to elevate the play of their teammates to championship greatness. Jordan was determined to dispel any such doubts and certainly did so in the 1990–91 through 1992–93 seasons. Not only did Jordan dedicate himself to winning multiple championships, but he did so by adhering to the Bulls' Triangle Offense, which allowed his teammates to excel as well. At the end of the three years, Jordan ended up accomplishing something that Bird, Magic, and Isiah never did—-three straight rings.

One of the central figures in the Bulls dynasty was head coach Phil Jackson. The former NBA player and CBA coach joined the Bulls as an assistant coach in 1987, and was named head coach two years later.

Isiah Thomas averaged 27.6 points and earned 1990 Finals MVP honors in Detroit's five game triumph over the Portland Trail Blazers.

The sight of Scottie Pippen and Michael Jordan caused many a long night for Bulls opponents.

A Well-Oiled Machine

Isiah Thomas was fresh from leading Indiana University to the NCAA title when the 6-1 guard was selected by the Detroit Pistons with the No. 2 overall pick in the 1981 NBA Draft. In his rookie season, Thomas averaged 17 points and 7.8 assists, and soon established himself as one of the NBA's premier guards. The Pistons then hired Chuck Daly, a veteran college coach with some NBA experience. Daly instilled a defensive-minded philosophy and recruited new players—center Bill Laimbeer, forwards Dennis Rodman, Rick Mahorn, John Salley, Mark Aguirre, and guards Vinnie Johnson and Joe Dumars—who changed the game through their physical style of play. After winning the 1989 championship, the Pistons went on to defeat the Portland Trail Blazers in five games in the 1990 Finals.

Bullish Results

The Dynamic Duo. The Terrific Twosome. Whatever moniker was given to the team of Michael Jordan and Scottie Pippen, it certainly applied. The two teammates formed the NBA's premier one-two punch, wreaking havoc on the offensive and defensive ends of the floor. Pippen, the wiry, multi-dimensional 6-7 forward was a master ballhandler and one-on-one defender who served as the perfect complement to the high-flying, high-scoring 6-6 Jordan.

Drafted in 1992 by Orlando, Shaquille O'Neal led the Magic to the NBA Finals three years later.

Magical Impression

Few players entered the NBA with such fanfare as Shaquille O'Neal did in 1992. The Louisiana State sophomore was selected with the No. 1 overall pick by the Orlando Magic and earned NBA Player of the Week honors in his very first week of play, becoming the only rookie in league history to receive such an honor. The 7-1, 300-pound center was named NBA Rookie of the Year after he averaged 23.4 points and 13.9 rebounds.

CHAMPIONSHIP TEAMS

1989–90 Detroit Pistons

1990–91 Chicago Bulls

1991–92 Chicago Bulls

1992–93 Chicago Bulls

1993–1995

AFTER MICHAEL JORDAN ANNOUNCED his retirement prior to the 1993–94 NBA season, a collective sigh of relief was heard around the league—after Chicago's impressive championship three-peat, another team could finally have a chance to compete with the Bulls for the coveted Larry O'Brien Trophy. Enter Hakeem Olajuwon and the Houston Rockets. The balance of power quickly shifted from East to West as Olajuwon and the Rockets picked up where the Bulls left off by winning two consecutive titles. Meanwhile Patrick Ewing and Pat Riley turned the New York Knicks into contenders.

Championship Blast Off

The Houston Rockets already boasted a long list of great players who had left indelible marks on the game—Elvin Hayes, Rudy Tomjanovich, Calvin Murphy, Moses Malone— but only one would lead them to the NBA promised land: Hakeem Olajuwon. The 7-0, Nigerian-born All-Star certified his status as one of the NBA's greatest centers of all time after his brilliant performance during the 1993–94 season. Ten years after being selected with the No. 1 overall pick in the NBA Draft (ahead of Michael Jordan), Olajuwon sent the Rockets into orbit, leading them to the NBA championship while becoming the first player in NBA history to win the NBA MVP, NBA Defensive Player of the Year, and NBA Finals MVP awards in the same season. Olajuwon was reunited with his University of Houston Phi Slama Jama teammate Clyde Drexler the following season, and led the underdog Rockets from a sixth seed in the playoffs to their second straight NBA title, while once again picking up NBA Finals MVP honors. The Rockets became the fifth NBA franchise ever to win back-to-back titles.

Whether he was facing his opponents or dropping a series of fakes with any number of his back-to-the-basket moves, "Hakeem the Dream" Olajuwon consistently befuddled defenders.

The Houston Rockets won back-to-back NBA championship rings in 1994 and '95.

Known as a player's coach, Rudy Tomjanovich took over as head coach in 1992 and netted the city of Houston its first-ever championship three years later. The Rockets repeated the feat the next season.

Gotham's Championship Dreams

Madison Square Garden came to life in the 1990s as New York's beloved Knicks knocked on the NBA's championship door. Years of great expectations following the selection of center Patrick Ewing in the 1985 NBA Draft were finally realized as the Knicks elevated themselves into championship contender status. Atlantic Divison titles and 50-win seasons became the norm at the Garden as the Knicks battled the Chicago Bulls and Indiana Pacers year after year for Eastern Conference supremacy. The Knicks finally made their first NBA Finals appearance in 21 years when they met the Houston Rockets in the 1994 Finals. After nine years in the NBA, it was Ewing's first opportunity at the NBA ring. Although the Knicks lost to the Rockets in a thrilling seven-game series, Knicks pride officially returned to the Garden.

Patrick Ewing led a Garden party in New York as the Knicks advanced to the 1994 NBA Finals, their first appearance in 21 years.

Was Pat Riley really a great coach or was he simply a benefactor of the Hall of Fame talent that resulted in four NBA titles under his watch? Riley provided the answer as he scrapped the "Showtime" offense from his L.A. days and adopted a new physical defensive style of play that suited the Knicks' personnel to a tee. The result: three Atlantic Division titles, four 50-plus-win seasons, one NBA Finals appearance, and many memorable moments.

CHAMPIONSHIP TEAMS

1993–94 Houston Rockets

1994–95 Houston Rockets

1995–1997

THE STATEMENT WAS SHORT AND SWEET, yet spoke volumes: "I'm back." With two words faxed to news outlets on March 18, 1995, Michael Jordan unretired to lead the Chicago Bulls to three more championships. Meanwhile, Shaquille O'Neal moved to Los Angeles, John Stockton and Karl Malone ruled the Utah Jazz, and the NBA turned 50 with a bang, and went abroad. The formation of the WNBA was a significant close to three exciting years of basketball.

Shaq Goes Hollywood

The Los Angeles Lakers landed one of the biggest free-agent prizes in NBA history when Shaquille O'Neal agreed to a seven-year contract in July 1996. The All-Star center was the latest in the line of big men to wear the Lakers uniform. George Mikan, Wilt Chamberlain, and Kareem Abdul-Jabbar were among the greatest centers to play the game, and O'Neal welcomed the challenge of following in their footsteps. The signing was a lifelong dream for O'Neal who idolized Magic Johnson and the Showtime era of the '80s.

The arrival of O'Neal (left) and the draft rights to high-school phenom Kobe Bryant were big acquisitions for GM Jerry West.

The NBA at 50

The NBA tipped off its golden anniversary on October 29, 1996, when NBA Commissioner David Stern announced the 50 Greatest Players who, together with the Top 10 Coaches and Teams in NBA History, were chosen by a blue-ribbon panel of media, former players and coaches, and current and former general managers and executives. The celebration climaxed when 47 of the 50 greatest gathered during the 1997 All-Star Weekend in Cleveland (right).

The Messenger and the Mailman

These two future Hall of Famers entered the NBA with virtually no fanfare. John Stockton was selected with the 16th overall pick of the 1984 NBA Draft, while Karl Malone was drafted by the Jazz with the 13th overall pick in 1985. Yet these players rewrote the NBA record book with Stockton becoming the NBA's all-time assists and steals king, and Malone challenging Kareem Abdul-Jabbar's all-time scoring record.

Thanks to Stockton and Malone, the Jazz reached the Western Conference Finals five times in a seven-year span and made back-to-back NBA Finals appearances in 1997 and '98. Malone, who won two NBA MVP awards in the 1990s, has a special fondness for a man he would call a teammate for 18 seasons: "There absolutely, positively, will never ever be another John Stockton—ever."

John Stockton and Karl Malone were the epitome of consistency. The Utah Jazz tandem ran the pick and roll to perfection, racking up plenty of points and assists in the process, while leading the Jazz to the playoffs every season.

CHAMPIONSHIP TEAMS

1995–96 Chicago Bulls

1996–97 Chicago Bulls

Jason Williams (#55) of the Sacramento Kings passes to his teammate around Rasho Nesterovic (#8) of the Minnesota Timberwolves during the 1999 Japan Games at the Tokyo Dome in Japan.

Lisa Leslie (left), Sheryl Swoopes (kneeling), and Rebecca Lobo were among the first three players to join the WNBA, which tipped off its inaugural season on June 21, 1997.

A League of Their Own

Women's college basketball was surging in popularity as attendance and television ratings grew considerably. Record numbers of fans turned out to support their favorite college teams and, together with the success of the 1996 US Women's Olympic team in Atlanta, the obvious was confirmed: the timing was right to launch a women's professional basketball league.

On April 24, 1996, the NBA's Board of Governors approved the Women's National Basketball Association and their catch-phrase, "We Got Next," hit the world. Val Ackerman, the former University of Virginia All-American, was named President of the WNBA on August 7, 1996, and less than one year later, eight teams tipped off the inaugural season. The women's league became an instant success and welcomed its 10-millionth fan five years later.

Global Impact

The NBA's global popularity continued to grow as the league routinely sent teams overseas to showcase their talents in regular-season contests. Fan and media support for these games proved to be extraordinary. In 1996, the New Jersey Nets played the Orlando Magic in two games and drew more than 75,000 fans to the Tokyo Dome, while the Minnesota Timberwolves and Sacramento Kings played a two-game series two years later at the same venue. Sold-out crowds wore jerseys of their favorite teams and held homemade signs welcoming their basketball heroes. NBA players were floored by the tremendous amount of enthusiasm displayed by these international fans.

1997–1999

AS THE DECADE DREW TO A CLOSE, so did the Chicago Bulls' glorious championship run of six titles in eight seasons. The success and dominance of the Bulls in the 1990s invited comparisons to the greatest dynasty of them all, the Boston Celtics. While one champion faded, the NBA welcomed a new one in 1999, as the San Antonio Spurs became the first former ABA team to win a title. It also officially marked the arrival of Tim Duncan as the league's newest superstar, who took home NBA Finals MVP honors in only his second season. Meanwhile, A. C. Green became basketball's new Iron Man and Allan Houston's game-winning shot brought the Knicks to the championship series.

BASKETBALL'S IRON MAN

On November 20, 1997, Dallas Maverick A. C. Green became the NBA's newest Iron Man, breaking the 906-game streak of Randy Smith's (right), who had scored 16,262 points for a 16.7 points-per-game average during his 12 years in the NBA. Cal Ripken (left), Major League Baseball's Iron Man who played in 2,632 consecutive games, was also on hand to celebrate A. C. Green's record achievement of 907 straight games.

The Ultimate Curtain Call

When it appeared Michael Jordan couldn't possibly outdo himself when it came to delivering dramatic moments, he managed to do the unthinkable in sinking perhaps the greatest clutch basket of his exemplary career. The stage was set as the Chicago Bulls trailed the Utah Jazz in Game 6 of the 1998 NBA Finals. A loss to the Jazz meant a Game 7 showdown in the hostile Delta Center. Down by three points with less than a minute remaining, Jordan seized control of the game, first scoring on a drive to the basket and then instantly following up by stripping the ball from Karl Malone. Jordan dribbled the ball up the court as the sold-out crowd stood in pained anticipation of what No. 23 would do next—which was nail a 20-footer with 5.2 seconds left in regulation. The basket gave the Bulls an 87-86 victory, another title, and the ultimate storybook ending to Jordan's brilliant career. Six months later, Jordan announced his retirement from the Chicago Bulls for the second time.

What a Finish

The eighth-seeded New York Knicks' 1999 storybook playoff run picked up momentum when Allan Houston sank a running layup that dropped at the buzzer of Game 5 of the first-round series, stunning the sold-out Miami Arena crowd. It was the third year in a row that the Heat had lost to the Knicks in the playoffs. New York continued its unlikely postseason run all the way to the NBA Finals and, in the process, became the first eighth-seeded team in NBA history to advance to the championship series. Perhaps even more impressive was the fact that they did so even without Patrick Ewing, who was sidelined with a wrist injury. New heroes such as Latrell Sprewell, Marcus Camby, and Houston carried the load for the Knicks, who fell just short of championship glory.

Michael the Magnificent struck again, breaking the hearts of Jazz fans everywhere when he nailed the Game 6 winner of the 1998 NBA Finals.

Championship Spurs

When it came to individual accolades, few could touch David Robinson's basketball résumé. The Admiral won virtually every award imaginable, including NBA MVP, Defensive Player of the Year, NBA Rookie of the Year, two Olympic gold medals, All-NBA, and All-NBA Defensive Team honors. Yet one special award seemed to elude him after eight seasons in the league: the Larry O'Brien Championship Trophy. Then rookie Tim Duncan joined the Spurs for the 1997–98 season. Robinson willingly took a backseat so Duncan could flourish. The move paid off and, after playing only two seasons together, they celebrated their first NBA title—together.

CHAMPIONSHIP TEAMS

1997–98 Chicago Bulls

1998–99 San Antonio Spurs

Individual Honors

1989–90

Scoring Leader:
Michael Jordan, Chicago (33.6)
Rebound Leader:
Hakeem Olajuwon, Houston (14.0)
Assist Leader:
John Stockton, Utah (14.5)
Free-Throw Percentage Leader:
Larry Bird, Boston (.930)
Steal Leader:
Michael Jordan, Chicago (2.77)
Blocked-Shot Leader:
Hakeem Olajuwon, Houston (4.59)
Three-Point Percentage Leader:
Steve Kerr, Cleveland (.507)
MVP: Magic Johnson,
Los Angeles Lakers
Rookie of the Year:
David Robinson, San Antonio
Coach of the Year:
Pat Riley, Los Angeles Lakers
NBA Finals MVP:
Isiah Thomas, Detroit
Defensive Player of the Year:
Dennis Rodman, Detroit
Sixth Man Award:
Ricky Pierce, Milwaukee
Most Improved Player:
Rony Seikaly, Miami
Hall of Fame Class:
David Bing, Player
Elvin E. Hayes, Player
Donald Neil Johnston, Player
Vernon Earl Monroe, Player

1990–91

Scoring Leader:
Michael Jordan, Chicago (31.5)
Rebound Leader:
David Robinson, San Antonio (13.0)
Assist Leader:
John Stockton, Utah (14.2)
Free-Throw Percentage Leader:
Reggie Miller, Indiana (.918)

Steal Leader:
Alvin Robertson, Milwaukee (3.04)
Blocked-Shot Leader:
Hakeem Olajuwon, Houston (3.95)
Three-Point Percentage Leader:
Jim Les, Sacramento (.461)
MVP: Michael Jordan, Chicago
Rookie of the Year:
Derrick Coleman, New Jersey
Coach of the Year:
Don Chaney, Houston
NBA Finals MVP:
Michael Jordan, Chicago
Defensive Player of the Year:
Dennis Rodman, Detroit
Sixth Man Award:
Detlef Schrempf, Indiana
Most Improved Player:
Scott Skiles, Orlando
Hall of Fame Class:
Nathaniel Archibald, Player
David W. Cowens, Player
Lawrence Fleisher, Contributor
Harry J. Gallatin, Player
Robert M. Knight, Coach
Lawrence F. O'Brien, Contributor
Borislav Stankovic, Contributor

1991–92

Scoring Leader:
Michael Jordan, Chicago (30.1)
Rebound Leader:
Dennis Rodman, Detroit (18.7)
Assist Leader:
John Stockton, Utah (13.7)
Free-Throw Percentage Leader:
Mark Price, Cleveland (.947)
Steal Leader:
John Stockton, Utah (2.98)
Blocked-Shot Leader:
David Robinson, San Antonio (4.49)
Three-Point Percentage Leader:
Dana Barros, Seattle (.446)
MVP: Michael Jordan, Chicago

Rookie of the Year:
Larry Johnson, Charlotte
Coach of the Year:
Don Nelson, Golden State
NBA Finals MVP:
Michael Jordan, Chicago
Defensive Player of the Year:
David Robinson, San Antonio
Sixth Man Award:
Detlef Schrempf, Indiana
Most Improved Player:
Pervis Ellison, Washington
Hall of Fame Class:
Sergei Belov, Player
Louis P. Carnesecca, Coach
Cornelius L. Hawkins, Player
Robert J. Lanier, Player
Alfred J. McGuire, Coach
John (Jack) T. Ramsay, Coach
Lusia Harris-Stewart, Player
Nera D. White, Player
Phillip D. Woolpert, Coach

1992–93

Scoring Leader:
Michael Jordan, Chicago (32.6)
Rebound Leader:
Dennis Rodman, Detroit (18.3)
Assist Leader:
John Stockton, Utah (12.0)
Free-Throw Percentage Leader:
Mark Price, Cleveland (.948)
Steal Leader:
Michael Jordan, Chicago (2.83)
Blocked-Shot Leader:
Hakeem Olajuwon, Houston (4.17)
Three-Point Percentage Leader:
B.J. Armstrong, Chicago (.453)
MVP: Charles Barkley, Phoenix
Rookie of the Year:
Shaquille O'Neal, Orlando
Coach of the Year:
Pat Riley, New York
NBA Finals MVP:
Michael Jordan, Chicago

Defensive Player of the Year:
Hakeem Olajuwon, Houston
Sixth Man Award:
Clifford Robinson, Portland
Most Improved Player:
Mahmoud Abdul-Rauf, Denver
Hall of Fame Class:
Walter Bellamy, Player
Julius W. Erving, Player
Daniel P. Issel, Player
Ann E. Meyers, Player
Richard S. McGuire, Player
Calvin J. Murphy, Player
Uljana Semjonova, Player
William T. Walton, Player

1993–94

Scoring Leader:
David Robinson,
San Antonio (29.8)
Rebound Leader:
Dennis Rodman, San Antonio (17.3)
Assist Leader:
John Stockton, Utah (12.6)
Free-Throw Percentage Leader:
Mahmoud Abdul-Rauf,
Denver (.956)
Steal Leader:
Nate McMillan, Seattle (2.96)
Blocked-Shot Leader:
Dikembe Mutombo, Denver (4.10)
Three-Point Percentage Leader:
Tracy Murray, Portland (.459)
MVP: Hakeem Olajuwon,
Houston
Rookie of the Year:
Chris Webber, Golden State
Coach of the Year:
Lenny Wilkens, Atlanta
NBA Finals MVP:
Hakeem Olajuwon, Houston
Defensive Player of the Year:
Hakeem Olajuwon, Houston
Sixth Man Award:
Dell Curry, Charlotte

Most Improved Player:
Don MacLean, Washington
Hall of Fame Class:
Carol Blazejowski, Player
Denzil (Denny) E. Crum, Coach
Charles J. Daly, Coach
Harry (Buddy) Jeannette, Player
Cesare Rubini, Coach

1994–95

Scoring Leader:
Shaquille O'Neal, Orlando (29.3)
Rebound Leader:
Dennis Rodman,
San Antonio (16.8)
Assist Leader:
John Stockton, Utah (12.3)
Free-Throw Percentage Leader:
Spud Webb, Sacramento (.934)
Steal Leader:
Scottie Pippen, Chicago (2.94)
Blocked-Shot Leader:
Dikembe Mutombo, Denver (3.91)
Three-Point Percentage Leader:
Steve Kerr, Chicago (.524)
MVP: David Robinson,
San Antonio
Rookies of the Year:
Grant Hill, Detroit and
Jason Kidd, Dallas
Coach of the Year:
Del Harris, Los Angeles Lakers
NBA Finals MVP:
Hakeem Olajuwon, Houston
Defensive Player of the Year:
Dikembe Mutombo, Denver
Sixth Man Award:
Anthony Mason, New York
Most Improved Player:
Dana Barros, Philadelphia
Hall of Fame Class:
Anne Donovan, Player
Aleksandr Gomelsky, Coach
Kareem Abdul-Jabbar, Player
John Kundla, Coach
Vern Mikkelsen, Player
Cheryl Miller, Player
Earl Strom, Referee

1995–96

Scoring Leader:
Michael Jordan, Chicago (30.4)
Rebound Leader:
Dennis Rodman, Chicago (14.9)
Assist Leader:
John Stockton, Utah (11.2)
Free-Throw Percentage Leader:
Mahmoud Abdul-Rauf,
Denver (.930)
Steal Leader:
Gary Payton, Seattle (2.85)
Blocked-Shot Leader:
Dikembe Mutombo, Denver (4.49)
Three-Point Percentage Leader:
Tim Legler, Washington (.522)
MVP: Michael Jordan, Chicago
Rookie of the Year:
Damon Stoudamire, Toronto
Coach of the Year:
Phil Jackson, Chicago
NBA Finals MVP:
Michael Jordan, Chicago
Defensive Player of the Year:
Gary Payton, Seattle
Sixth Man Award:
Toni Kukoc, Chicago
Most Improved Player:
Gheorghe Muresan, Washington
Hall of Fame Class:
Kresimir Cosic, Player
George Gervin, Player
Gail Goodrich, Player
Nancy Lieberman, Player
David Thompson, Player
George Yardley, Player

1996–97

Scoring Leader:
Michael Jordan, Chicago (29.6)
Rebound Leader:
Dennis Rodman, Chicago (16.1)
Assist Leader:
Mark Jackson, Denver/Indiana (11.4)
Free-Throw Percentage Leader:
Mark Price, Golden State (.906)
Steal Leader:
Mookie Blaylock, Atlanta (2.72)

Blocked-Shot Leader:
Shawn Bradley,
New Jersey/Dallas (3.40)
Three-Point Percentage Leader:
Glen Rice, Charlotte (.470)
MVP: Karl Malone, Utah
Rookie of the Year:
Allen Iverson, Philadelphia
Coach of the Year:
Pat Riley, Miami
NBA Finals MVP:
Michael Jordan, Chicago
Defensive Player of the Year:
Dikembe Mutombo, Atlanta
Sixth Man Award:
John Starks, New York
Most Improved Player:
Isaac Austin, Miami
Hall of Fame Class:
Pete Carril, Coach
Joan Crawford, Player
Denise Curry, Player
Antonio Diaz-Miguel, Coach
Alex English, Player
Don Haskins, Coach
Bailey Howell, Player

1997–98

Scoring Leader:
Michael Jordan, Chicago (28.7)
Rebound Leader:
Dennis Rodman, Chicago (15.0)
Assist Leader:
Rod Strickland, Washington (10.5)
Free-Throw Percentage Leader:
Chris Mullin, Indiana (.939)
Steal Leader:
Mookie Blaylock, Atlanta (2.61)
Blocked-Shot Leader:
Marcus Camby, Toronto (3.65)
Three-Point Percentage Leader:
Dale Ellis, Seattle (.464)
MVP: Michael Jordan, Chicago
Rookie of the Year:
Tim Duncan, San Antonio
Coach of the Year:
Larry Bird, Indiana
NBA Finals MVP:
Michael Jordan, Chicago

Defensive Player of the Year:
Dikembe Mutombo, Atlanta
Sixth Man Award:
Danny Manning, Phoenix
Most Improved Player:
Alan Henderson, Atlanta
Hall of Fame Class:
Larry Bird, Player
Jody Conradt, Coach
Alexander (Alex) Hannum, Coach
Marques Haynes, Player
Aleksandar Nikolic, Coach
Arnold (Arnie) Risen, Player
Leonard (Lenny) Wilkens, Coach

1998–99

Scoring Leader:
Allen Iverson, Philadelphia (26.8)
Rebound Leader:
Chris Webber, Sacramento (13.0)
Assist Leader:
Jason Kidd, Phoenix (10.8)
Free-Throw Percentage Leader:
Reggie Miller, Indiana (.915)
Steal Leader:
Kendall Gill, New Jersey (2.68)
Blocked-Shot Leader:
Alonzo Mourning, Miami (3.91)
Three-Point Percentage Leader:
Dell Curry, Milwaukee (.476)
MVP: Karl Malone, Utah
Rookie of the Year:
Vince Carter, Toronto
Coach of the Year:
Mike Dunleavy, Portland
NBA Finals MVP:
Tim Duncan, San Antonio
Defensive Player of the Year:
Alonzo Mourning, Miami
Sixth Man Award:
Darrell Armstrong, Orlando
Most Improved Player:
Darrell Armstrong, Orlando
Hall of Fame Class:
Wayne Embry, Contributor
Kevin McHale, Player
Billie Moore, Coach
John Thompson, Coach
Fred Zollner, Contributor

2000

THE 21ST CENTURY WELCOMED new NBA champions and said goodbye to some of the game's biggest legends. Phil Jackson arrived in Los Angeles prior to the start of the 1999–2000 season and proved why he belongs on the short list of greatest coaches ever, guiding the Lakers to one of the best seasons in franchise history. Shaquille O'Neal enjoyed an MVP campaign in leading the Lakers to their 12th NBA title, this time against the Indiana Pacers and frustrating their hopes of sending head coach Larry Bird off into the sunset with a championship ring. Charles Barkley put the finishing touches on his Hall of Fame career, although an injury allowed him to see action in only 20 games.

CHAMPIONSHIP TEAM

1999–2000 Los Angeles Lakers

THE CHAMPIONSHIP DIFFERENCE: PHIL JACKSON

At the start of the new century, Phil Jackson was one of the most decorated coaches in NBA history, yet questions still lingered. How great of a coach is he, the basketball critics wondered. Just how difficult was it to win six titles in eight seasons when Michael Jordan and Scottie Pippen are on your roster? Fortunately, Jackson would get the chance to show what a difference a future Hall of Fame coach can make when he took over the reins of the Los Angeles Lakers prior to the 1999–2000 season.

Enter the Lakers

Other than All-Stars Shaquille O'Neal and Kobe Bryant, the Lakers were a mystery to Jackson.

"There were times when I didn't know really if we had all that it took as

Kobe Bryant and Shaquille O'Neal were all smiles after leading the Lakers to the 2000 NBA championship. O'Neal capped off his regular-season MVP performance by winning Finals MVP honors as well.

a basketball team," Jackson admitted months into his first season with the Lakers.

Jackson modified the triangle-offense, the same offense he used in Chicago to great success, to utilize O'Neal's skills, and the results were impressive. Not only did O'Neal win his first NBA MVP Award, but the Lakers also compiled a 67-15 record en route to the franchise's first championship in 12 years.

"This has been a fairy-tale season for us," said Lakers owner Jerry Buss, "and I think you have to give a lot of the credit to Phil Jackson. The Lakers have evolved into a different team under Phil. They have a cohesiveness and motivation that was lacking before. I think you can attribute such a change to Phil's coaching. He has done just a great, great job."

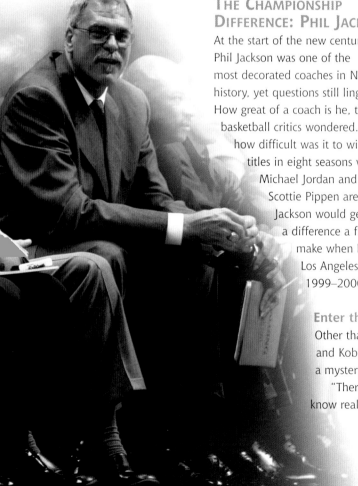

Phil Jackson once again proved his greatness as a coach in leading the Lakers to an NBA title in 2000.

BIRD SETS THE PACE IN INDY

The 1999--00 season was a breakthrough for the Indiana Pacers and also marked the end of Larry Bird's short coaching career. On May 12, 1997, Bird was named head coach of the Indiana Pacers even though he had never coached a game before. Yet the Pacers had no doubts about handing the reins to Bird.

The former Indiana State All-American and Boston Celtics star forward led the Pacers to their first-ever NBA Finals appearance in 2000. The Pacers, who had lost in the Eastern Conference Finals four times in the previous six seasons, were led by Jalen Rose and Reggie Miller. Rose led the team in scoring with an 18.2 average and picked up NBA Most Improved Player honors, while Miller averaged 18.1 points. The Pacers compiled an 11-6 playoff mark entering the NBA Finals where they met the Los Angeles Lakers.

After being down 2-1, the Pacers lost the pivotal Game 4 in overtime. Indy ended up losing the series in six games and Bird concluded his Pacers coaching career with a 147-67 record, along with two Central Division titles and one NBA Coach of the Year honor (1998).

"He pulls people together. When he talks, you come into his world. That's what a coach has to do," said Pacers President Donnie Walsh.

When Larry Bird speaks, players such as Reggie Miller listen. The three-time NBA champion with the Boston Celtics made his presence felt in Indy, guiding the Pacers to an NBA Finals appearance in 2000.

Charles Barkley (center) closed out his Hall of Fame career with the Houston Rockets, where he played for four seasons. Barkley's championship mission went unfulfilled despite having future Hall of Famers Clyde Drexler and Hakeem Olajuwon as teammates.

BARKLEY'S FAREWELL SEASON

The NBA said goodbye to one of the greatest and most outspoken players ever to put on a uniform. Unfortunately for Charles Barkley and his legions of fans, his farewell season ended prematurely. On December 8, 1999, the future Hall of Famer suffered a ruptured quadriceps tendon in his left knee during a Houston Rockets road game in Philadelphia, and it appeared he would be sidelined for the rest of the season.

However, Barkley was determined to leave the game on his own terms and, on April 19, 2000, he did just that. Barkley reappeared for the Rockets' final home game and said goodbye one last time.

The 1993 NBA MVP ended up joining Kareem Abdul-Jabbar, Wilt Chamberlain, and Karl Malone as just one of four players in NBA history to accumulate 20,000 points, 10,000 rebounds, and 4,000 assists.

Charles Barkley waves to the crowd as he walks off the court for the final time in Philadelphia after suffering a knee injury.

2001

THE 2000–01 SEASON featured breakout performances, with Allen Iverson, Ben Wallace, and Tracy McGrady rising to the forefront. Iverson was Mr. MVP, winning All-Star Game and regular-season honors, while Wallace provided much needed inside muscle for Detroit's defense. McGrady went from role player in Toronto to All-Star player in Orlando, and quickly emerged as one of the NBA's premier scorers. The National Basketball Development League tipped off its inaugural season in 2001, and the Greenville Groove were crowned league champions.

After making stops in Washington, DC, and Orlando, Ben Wallace found a home with the Pistons in 2000–01 and emerged as one of the NBA's premier defensive forces.

ALLEN IVERSON: LITTLE BIG MAN

2000–2001 was a memorable season for Allen Iverson and the Philadelphia 76ers, and it nearly culminated in a championship title. The 6-0 guard out of Georgetown University helped propel the Sixers to a 10-0 start, and they never looked back, boasting the Eastern Conference's best record at 56-26. Iverson not only captured his second scoring title by averaging 31.1 points; he also collected All-Star Game MVP honors and became the shortest player in NBA history to win the NBA MVP Award. Iverson went on to lead Philly to their first NBA Finals appearance in 18 years as the Sixers battled the Los Angeles Lakers before succumbing in five games.

A fearless competitor, Allen Iverson (right) is undaunted going to the basket against the likes of 7-1 Shaquille O'Neal.

FROM UNKNOWN TO ALL-STAR

Ben Wallace was not an overnight sensation. Wallace played two seasons at Cuyahoga Community College in Ohio before transferring to Virginia Union. After going undrafted in 1996, Wallace signed as a free agent with the Washington Bullets. Four seasons later, including one in Orlando, Wallace was traded to Detroit along with Chucky Atkins in 2000 for superstar Grant Hill. The deal appeared one-sided in Orlando's favor but injuries derailed Hill while Wallace immediately became a one-man show on defense. He led the league in blocks and rebounds in only his second season in Motown, quickly establishing himself as one of the NBA's premier defenders. The 2000–01 season would serve as a springboard for him to win back-to-back NBA Defensive Player of the Year Awards.

THE NATIONAL BASKETBALL DEVELOPMENT LEAGUE

The inaugural NBDL season tipped off on November 16, 2001, in a game between the North Charleston Lowgators and the Greenville Groove. The league allows players to develop their skills and provides NBA teams a source of talent. Nearly 30 players have been called up to the NBA since the league began. One of them, Chris Anderson, was called up by the Denver Nuggets on November 23, 2001, and developed into a valuable role player. He averaged 14.5 minutes per game for the Nuggets during the 2002–03 season, and even participated in the NBA's Slam Dunk Contest in 2004.

Also known as the D-League, it doesn't just give players the chance to develop skills—coaches, trainers, and referees have also gone on to the next level, being tabbed by NBA teams.

The NBDL tipped off in 2001, providing players, coaches, trainers, and referees with an opportunity to develop their skills.

The Greenville Groove celebrated the inaugural 2002 NBDL championship by defeating the Charleston Lowgators at the North Charleston Coliseum, 76-68.

T-MAC'S BREAKOUT SEASON

For three seasons, Tracy McGrady lurked in the shadows of his older cousin Vince Carter. Selected with the ninth overall pick in the 1997 NBA Draft, McGrady showed improvement in each of his three seasons with the Toronto Raptors, but it wasn't until McGrady was acquired by the Orlando Magic that he really blossomed.

"This kid's a star."

The 6-8 forward, along with another high-profile acquisition, Grant Hill, formed one of the NBA's most potent one-two combinations. When Hill was sidelined with an ankle injury after four games, McGrady took over. The fourth-year player posted career highs in points (26.8), rebounds (7.5), assists (4.6), steals (1.51), and minutes played (40.1) in a season. His .457 field-goal percentage, .355 three-point field-goal percentage, and .733 free-throw percentage were also career bests.

"He's so much better than I thought," said Hill, his proud teammate. "This kid's a star."

CHAMPIONSHIP TEAM

2000–01 Los Angeles Lakers

The 26.8 points per game average was the highest for a player younger than 22. It was also an 11-point jump from his average the previous season. Not only did McGrady make the first of many All-Star appearances, but his overall numbers earned him the NBA's Most Improved Player Award.

Tracy McGrady starred in his first season with the Orlando Magic.

2002

THE NBA LANDSCAPE WAS slowly changing as the 2001–02 season unfolded. International stars such as Steve Nash, Peja Stojakovic, and Dirk Nowitzki enjoyed breakout All-Star seasons, while Jason Kidd led the Nets' revival in the swamps of Jersey. The All-Star point guard infused the team with relentless energy en route to an Atlantic Division title and an NBA Finals berth. But the Los Angeles Lakers crushed the Nets' hopes for a fairy-tale ending when the Lakers became the third team in league history to win three titles in a row.

At 7-0, Dirk Nowitzki is a threat from three-point territory, just as he is from under the basket.

Peja Stojakovic rose to prominence in the 2001–02 season.

One of the quickest players in the league, Steve Nash emerged as one of the NBA's premier point guards.

Nash averaged 17.9 points and 7.7 assists and earned All-NBA third-team honors while his teammate Nowitzki developed into one of the NBA's best forwards averaging 23.4 points and shooting .397 percent from the three-point line. Both players helped lead Dallas to a franchise best 57-25 record and a second-round finish in the playoffs.

Stojakovic also made quite an impression, showing the world why he was considered one of the top shooters, as he became the first international player ever to win the three-point contest. It was part of a breakout weekend for the 6-9 forward who scored 11 points in the All-Star Game the next day.

INTERNATIONAL INVASION

International players took center stage in the 2001–02 season, making their mark as the league's new crop of rising stars. Dallas Mavericks Steve Nash of Canada and Dirk Nowitzki of Germany, and Sacramento King Peja Stojakovic of Serbia, all made their first-ever All-Star appearances.

INTERNATIONAL'S NO. 1

The 2002 NBA Draft ushered in a new era when the Houston Rockets selected Yao Ming of the Chinese Basketball Association with the No. 1 overall draft pick. The 7-6 center is the first player from an international basketball league to be the top overall draft selection in NBA history. He quickly became a star.

CHAMPIONSHIP TEAM

2001–02 Los Angeles Lakers

JASON KIDD: FRANCHISE PLAYER

The task was daunting: turn around a 26-56 team and, more importantly, change the attitude of players accustomed to losing year after year. The New Jersey Nets had just suffered their third consecutive losing season and missed the playoffs for the sixth time in the last seven years when Jason Kidd arrived in exchange for Stephon Marbury in a huge trade with the Phoenix Suns. Kidd did what many thought was impossible when he single-handedly turned the team's fortunes around with his all-around skills that allowed his

Shaquille O'Neal made the 2002 Finals his personal showcase as he manhandled the New Jersey Nets in the Lakers' four-game sweep. O'Neal set the record for most points in a four-game series with 145.

teammates to blossom. Kidd averaged 14.7 points, 9.9 assists, and 6.3 rebounds while leading New Jersey to a 50-32 record and an Atlantic Division title.

Kidd was a triple-double waiting to happen and had the rare ability to dominate a game even when he wasn't scoring a lot of points. The Cinderella season came to a halt when the L.A. Lakers swept the Nets for their third consecutive title.

Jason Kidd earned All-NBA First-Team honors in leading the Nets. The All-Star guard's effectiveness resulted in a lot of easy baskets for New Jersey.

CHAMPIONSHIP THREE-PEAT

The three-peat quest officially began on opening night of the 2001–02 season. Only two franchises, the Boston Celtics of the 1960s and the Chicago Bulls of the '90s, had ever won back-to-back-to-back titles, and L.A. wanted to place their name alongside them.

The Lakers got off to an impressive 16-1 start before stumbling when Shaquille O'Neal was sidelined with an arthritic toe. O'Neal ended up missing 15 games that season, and the Lakers went 7-8 without their All-Star center and 51-16 with him patrolling the lane.

The Lakers ripped through the first two rounds of the playoffs before meeting their match in the Western Conference Finals against the Sacramento Kings. In one of the all-time classic playoff games, the Lakers escaped with a 112-106 overtime victory and then swept the New Jersey Nets in the NBA Finals, officially minting them as the newest NBA dynasty.

2003

IT WAS THE END OF A GOLDEN ERA in the NBA as legends Michael Jordan, John Stockton, and David Robinson all retired at the end of the 2002–03 season. The three players totaled 72,793 points, 21,220 rebounds, 23,880 assists, and 8 NBA championships. But, in the 2003–04 season, the league also said hello to a pair of high-profile rookies named LeBron James and Carmelo Anthony, who made instant impacts on their respective teams. Kevin Garnett emerged as the league's best player, winning NBA MVP honors, while the NBA's global popularity continued to grow as it played games in Paris and Japan.

LEGENDARY GOODBYES

Two of the greatest players to ever play the game waved goodbye to a sport they dominated for nearly two decades. Michael Jordan closed out his brilliant career in a regular-season game in Philadelphia on April 16, 2003, which included a special pregame presentation when Julius Erving and Moses Malone presented the future Hall of Famer with a customized golf cart. For Jordan, the goal was to lead the Washington Wizards to the playoffs in his final season. Although this didn't happen, the six-time champion could at least find comfort in leaving the game on his own terms.

As could John Stockton, who had been a model of consistent excellence as he and his teammate, Karl Malone, helped lead the Utah Jazz to 18 consecutive playoff appearances. The soft-spoken Spokane, Washington, native retired as the NBA all-time assists and steals leader, having been named to the All-Defensive Second Team five times. His career ended after the Jazz lost in the first round of the playoffs to the Kings.

John Stockton walked off the court for the last time upon the conclusion of Game 5 of the First Round of the NBA Playoffs, as the Utah Jazz lost the series to the Sacramento Kings.

Michael Jordan received a Brotherly Love sendoff from the Philadelphia fans who thanked the legend for his contributions in his final regular-season game.

THE ADMIRAL SETS SAIL

It was the ultimate retirement party for one of the game's greatest players when David Robinson received a championship curtain call with 35.6 seconds remaining in Game 6 of the 2003 NBA Finals. Fittingly, the 37-year-old center played a key role in the Spurs' clinching victory against the resilient New Jersey Nets. Robinson drew two charges in the third quarter and grabbed seven rebounds in the final seven minutes to help seal San Antonio's second championship win in five years, as teammate Tim Duncan picked up NBA Finals MVP honors.

"I'm just thrilled that David ended his career with a game like that," said Spurs head coach Gregg Popovich. "His effort was really wonderful. He really dug down deep and showed how important it was to him to help us get this victory."

CHAMPIONSHIP TEAM

2002–03 San Antonio Spurs

GLOBAL PRESENCE

The 2003–04 season began with an international flavor as NBA teams traveled outside North America to continue a long tradition of promoting the league by playing abroad.

The San Antonio Spurs played the Memphis Grizzlies in the NBA Europe Games at Bercy Arena in Paris, France, during the preseason, while the Los Angeles Clippers and Seattle SuperSonics tipped off the 2003–04 campaign with back-to-back games at the Saitama Super Arena in Saitama, Japan.

In 1990, the NBA had become the first major American sports league to play regular-season games abroad, when the Utah Jazz and Phoenix Suns played two games at the Metropolitan Gym in Tokyo, Japan.

Elton Brand of the Los Angeles Clippers walks through Chinzan-so garden in Tokyo, Japan.

MVP PERFORMANCE

Kevin Garnett was selected with the fifth overall pick in the 1995 NBA Draft by the Minnesota Timberwolves. A 6-11 senior out of Farragut Academy in Chicago, he possessed raw skills with enormous potential.

Less than two years later, Kevin Garnett was an NBA All-Star. The South Carolina native enjoyed his finest season as a pro in 2003–04, as he led the Minnesota Timberwolves to a franchise best 58-24 mark. Garnett earned MVP honors, posting career highs in points (24.2), rebounds (13.9), and averaging five assists and two blocks per game. Garnett received 120 out of 123 first-place votes in winning the award.

Kevin Garnett was Mr. Everything for the Timberwolves, playing different positions from small forward, to center, to even point guard in 2003–04.

ROOKIE SENSATIONS

By all accounts, rookies LeBron James of the Cleveland Cavaliers and Carmelo Anthony of the Denver Nuggets surpassed the loftiest of expectations. Both players proved instrumental in their respective teams' improvement as the Cavs saw their victory total jump from 17 wins to 35, while the Nuggets went from lottery team to playoff team.

James earned got milk? NBA Rookie of the Year honors as he joined NBA legends Oscar Robertson and Michael Jordan as the only players in NBA history to average more than 20 points, five rebounds, and five assists per game in their rookie season.

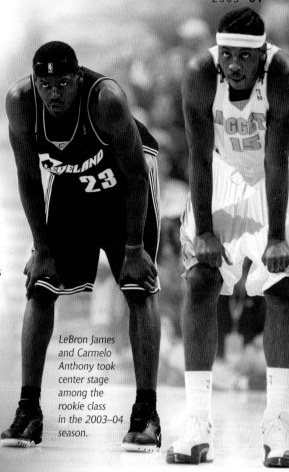

LeBron James and Carmelo Anthony took center stage among the rookie class in the 2003–04 season.

A WORLD GAME

The first Basketball Without Borders event was in 2001, when NBA players from the former Yugoslavia worked with 50 of their countries' children in Treviso, Italy. A basketball instructional camp that promotes leadership, education, sportsmanship, and healthy living, BWB also has seminars on social issues such as AIDS education. In 2004, the NBA and FIBA had camps in Europe, Latin America, and Africa.

Individual Honors

1999–2000

Scoring Leader:
Shaquille O'Neal,
Los Angeles Lakers (29.7)

Rebound Leader:
Dikembe Mutombo, Atlanta (14.1)

Assist Leader:
Jason Kidd, Phoenix (10.1)

Free-Throw Percentage Leader:
Jeff Hornacek, Utah (.950)

Steal Leader:
Eddie Jones, Charlotte (2.67)

Blocked-Shot Leader:
Alonzo Mourning, Miami (3.72)

Three-Point Percentage Leader:
Hubert Davis, Dallas (.491)

MVP: Shaquille O'Neal,
Los Angeles Lakers

Rookies of the Year:
Elton Brand, Chicago and
Steve Francis, Houston

Coach of the Year:
Glenn "Doc" Rivers, Orlando

NBA Finals MVP:
Shaquille O'Neal,
Los Angeles Lakers

Defensive Player of the Year:
Alonzo Mourning, Miami

Sixth Man Award:
Rodney Rogers, Phoenix

Most Improved Player:
Jalen Rose, Indiana

Hall of Fame Class:
Danny Biasone, Contributor
Robert McAdoo, Player
Charles Newton, Contributor
Pat Head Summitt, Coach
Isiah Thomas, Player
Morgan Wootten, Coach

2000–2001

Scoring Leader:
Allen Iverson, Philadelphia (31.1)

Rebound Leader:
Dikembe Mutombo,
Atlanta/Philadelphia (13.5)

Assist Leader:
Jason Kidd, Phoenix (9.8)

Free-Throw Percentage Leader:
Reggie Miller, Indiana (.928)

Steal Leader:
Allen Iverson, Philadelphia (2.51)

Blocked-Shot Leader:
Theo Ratliff,
Philadelphia (3.74)

**Three-Point
Percentage Leader:**
Brent Barry, Seattle
(.476)

MVP: Allen Iverson, Philadelphia

Rookie of the Year:
Mike Miller, Orlando

Coach of the Year:
Larry Brown, Philadelphia

NBA Finals MVP:
Shaquille O'Neal,
Los Angeles Lakers

Defensive Player of the Year:
Dikembe Mutombo, Philadelphia

Sixth Man Award:
Aaron McKie, Philadelphia

Most Improved Player:
Tracy McGrady, Orlando

Hall of Fame Class:
John Chaney, Coach
Mike Krzyzewski, Coach
Moses Malone, Player

2001–2002

Scoring Leader:
Allen Iverson, Philadelphia (31.4)
Rebound Leader:
Ben Wallace, Detroit (13.0)
Assist Leader:
Andre Miller,
Cleveland (10.9)
**Free-Throw
Percentage Leader:**
Reggie Miller,
Indiana (.911)
Steal Leader:
Allen Iverson,
Philadelphia (2.80)
Blocked-Shot Leader:
Ben Wallace, Detroit (3.48)
**Three-Point Percentage
Leader:**
Steve Smith,
San Antonio (.472)
MVP:
Tim Duncan,
San Antonio
Rookie of the Year:
Pau Gasol, Memphis
Coach of the Year:
Rick Carlisle,
Detroit

NBA Finals MVP:
Shaquille O'Neal,
Los Angeles Lakers
Defensive Player of the Year:
Ben Wallace, Detroit
Sixth Man Award:
Corliss Williamson, Detroit
Most Improved Player:
Jermaine O'Neal, Indiana
Hall of Fame Class:
 Harlem Globetrotters, Team
   Larry Brown, Coach
     Earvin "Magic"
       Johnson, Player
       Lute Olson, Coach
       Drazen Petrovic, Player
       Kay Yow, Coach

2002–2003

Scoring Leader:
Tracy McGrady, Orlando (32.1)
Rebound Leader:
Ben Wallace, Detroit (15.4)
Assist Leader:
Jason Kidd, New Jersey (8.9)
Free-Throw Percentage Leader:
Allan Houston, New York (.919)
Steal Leader:
Allen Iverson, Philadelphia (2.74)
Blocked-Shot Leader:
Theo Ratliff, Atlanta (3.23)
Three-Point Percentage Leader:
Bruce Bowen, San Antonio (.441)
MVP: Tim Duncan, San Antonio
Rookie of the Year:
Amaré Stoudemire, Phoenix
Coach of the Year:
Gregg Popovich, San Antonio
NBA Finals MVP:
Tim Duncan, San Antonio
Defensive Player of the Year:
Ben Wallace, Detroit
Sixth Man Award:
Bobby Jackson, Sacramento
Most Improved Player:
Gilbert Arenas, Golden State
Hall of Fame Class:
Leon Barmore, Coach
Chick Hearn, Contributor
Meadowlark Lemon, Contributor
Earl Lloyd, Contributor
Dino Meneghin, Player
Robert Parish, Player
James Worthy, Player

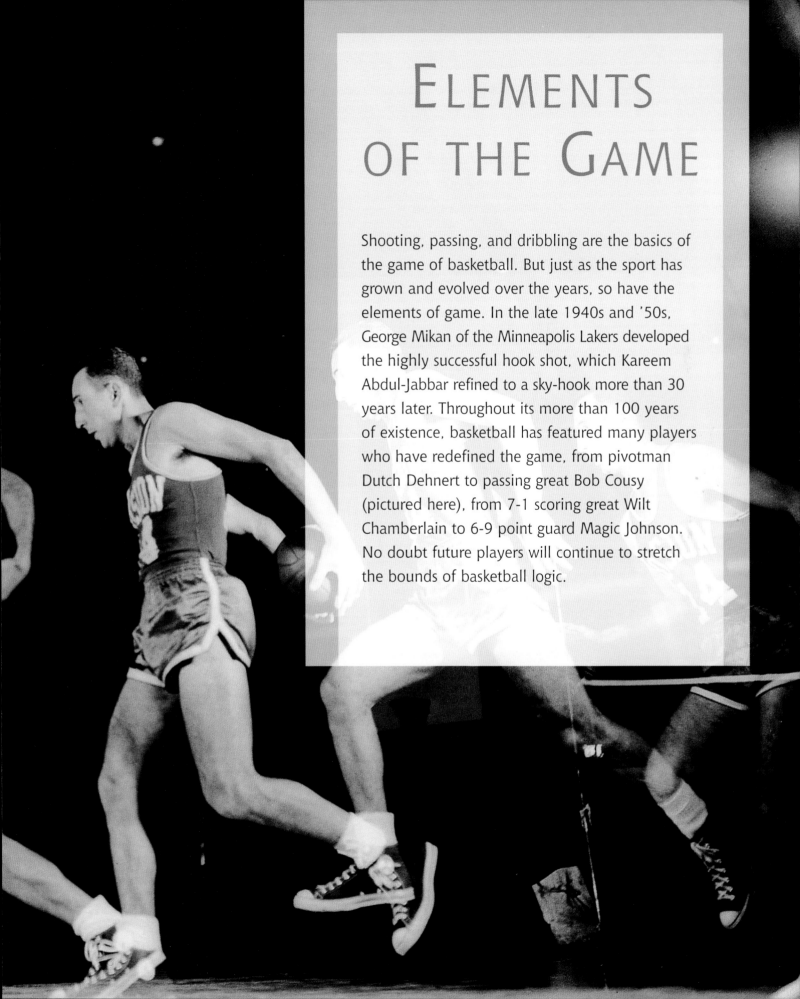

ELEMENTS OF THE GAME

Shooting, passing, and dribbling are the basics of the game of basketball. But just as the sport has grown and evolved over the years, so have the elements of game. In the late 1940s and '50s, George Mikan of the Minneapolis Lakers developed the highly successful hook shot, which Kareem Abdul-Jabbar refined to a sky-hook more than 30 years later. Throughout its more than 100 years of existence, basketball has featured many players who have redefined the game, from pivotman Dutch Dehnert to passing great Bob Cousy (pictured here), from 7-1 scoring great Wilt Chamberlain to 6-9 point guard Magic Johnson. No doubt future players will continue to stretch the bounds of basketball logic.

The Innovators

BASKETBALL—THE NAME SAYS IT ALL. The object of the game is to put the ball into the basket. More than 110 years after the sport's invention, the methods are different but the goal remains the same. What began as a wintertime distraction for a rambunctious group of students has evolved into a global phenomenon. How did basketball go from a curiosity to a worldwide sensation? Maybe the fans should be credited. Within five years of its conception in 1891, the sport was popular enough to support professional teams. A few early players had skills that particularly stood out, such as Kenny Sailors, Barney Sedran, and Dutch Dehnert.

Author, minister, professor— although he had many titles, Naismith will be remembered as the inventor of basketball.

THE FOUNDING FATHER

Fearing the mischief that would result from another long winter of students confined indoors, school administrators gave physical-education instructor James Naismith 14 days to create a new indoor sport. As the deadline neared, he remembered a game from his childhood in Canada called duck-on-a-rock, in which players threw small stones at a target sitting atop a large boulder. He also remembered an exercise he had devised for rugby players at Montreal's McGill University, where the athletes flipped a ball into a box to stay in shape during the winter. He combined elements of both into a game he called "basket ball," which would be played according to 13 rules he drafted.

THE FIRST GAME

On December 21, 1891, 18 students from Naismith's gymnastics class played the first basketball game on a court 50 feet long and 35 feet wide in the YMCA gym. The goal was to put a soccer ball into one of two peach baskets, 10 feet from the ground. "There were three forwards, three centers, and three backs on each team," recalled Naismith years later. "I chose two of the center men to jump, then threw the ball between them. It was the start of the first basketball game and the finish of trouble with that class."

William R. Chase made the first basket in history on a 25-foot shot from midcourt. It also proved to be the only basket in the game, which ended 1-0.

Early games, such as this one from the 1890s, moved at a slower pace because the players had to use a ladder to retrieve the ball after every completed shot.

The New York Whirlwinds, led by Barney Sedran (left) and Marty Friedman (sitting left), were one of the best pro teams during the early 1920s.

THE FIRST PROS

Naismith's invention quickly became popular—too popular. In 1896, the YMCA began limiting the number of basketball games in its gyms because the sport was crowding out other activities, and because it had become too rough. Rather than cancel games, the Trenton Basketball Team moved to a new location and charged admission. On November 7, 1896, Trenton hosted the Brooklyn YMCA at the Masonic Temple, and so many fans attended that the club had enough money left over to pay the players.

The first professional league was formed two years later in Philadelphia, and although the National Basketball League lasted only five years (1898–1903), many more pro basketball circuits would soon follow, including the BAA, the precursor to the NBA, and the ABA.

A JUMP FORWARD

Basketball may be mostly airborne today, but for the first 50 years of its history, the sport was grounded. Coaches preached two-handed set shots with feet planted on the floor, and frowned upon jump shots.

Kenny Sailors made history with his jump shot, which he developed out of necessity.

Kenny Sailors helped change that. As a boy growing up in Wyoming during the 1930s, he played basketball with his brother, Bud, who was four years older and much taller. Bud blocked almost all his shots until Kenny, out of desperation, began jumping just to get a shot off, and he became quite good at it. Sailors took his jump shot to the University of Wyoming, where he led the Cowboys to the 1943 NCAA title.

After service in the US Marine Corps, Sailors joined the Basketball Association of America in 1946 and became the first pro player to regularly use the jump shot.

THE HEAVENLY TWINS

At 5-4, Barney Sedran did not look like a basketball player—but he could shoot. In 1914, Sedran made 17 field goals in a game, all from long range (25–30 feet, by some accounts), into a hoop that didn't even have a backboard.

Sedran played in pro basketball's rough-and-tumble early days, when cages protected the players from the fans but not from each other. He teamed with long-time friend and backcourt mate Max "Marty" Friedman to make Utica a powerhouse in 1913–14, after which the "Heavenly Twins" joined Carbondale (Pennsylvania) and led the team to 35 straight wins in 1914–15. After Friedman returned from military service, the duo combined to make the New York Whirlwinds one of pro basketball's top teams during the early 1920s.

With Dutch Dehnert in the pivot, fans flocked to see the precision passing and cutting of the Original Celtics.

Rejected by his high-school team as too small, Barney Sedran played as a pro until 1927, then served as a coach until 1946.

MR. PIVOT

Henry "Dutch" Dehnert played professionally for more than 20 years (1917–1939), before becoming a successful coach during the 1940s. But he will forever be remembered as Mr. Pivot, the man who revolutionized basketball by turning his back to the hoop.

During the 1920s, Dehnert played for the Original Celtics. Opponents were thwarting the Celtics' fast break by leaving one player back on defense at all times. During a game in 1926, Dehnert devised a solution: he stood in front of the defender with his back to the basket. A guard passed him the ball, and Dehnert waited to pass to a teammate cutting to the basket. If the defender reached for the ball, Dehnert simply spun the other way for an easy basket.

The Shooting Innovators

THE PREMIER SHOOTERS IN THE NBA brim with confidence. The best ones can come into town and (routinely) break hearts, as Dr. J did in the 1970s with his dunking skills or Reggie Miller continues to do with his three-pointers. And the big men have their shots too, such as Kareem Abdul-Jabbar and his magical sky-hook. It wasn't always this way, however. During basketball's first five decades, almost everybody attempted two-handed set shots. Then came one-handed running shots, jump shots, dunks, sky-hooks, and three-point shots. All start out differently but end up in the same place—the basket. But the journey is half the fun.

ELEVATING THE GAME

The jump shot, a staple of modern basketball, hasn't changed much since its introduction. The player sets up facing the basket and waits for the ball on the perimeter, or he dribbles around a screen, before leaping into the air and releasing the shot from above his head.

The jump shot is so popular because it is difficult to defend. The shooter releases the ball high and, unless he can time his jump with that of the shooter, the defender has no chance to block it. For a small guard, tossing up a jump shot can be the best response to a center's height or a forward's muscle.

Kenny Sailors, who played for Wyoming, developed the shot in the 1940s; Joe Fulks took it further in the 1950s; and today it's practiced by almost every NBA player.

CHANGE— SINGLE-HANDEDLY

For eight-year-old Angelo "Hank" Luisetti, the two-handed set shot didn't work—he just couldn't get the ball to the hoop. So Luisetti took a step back and shot one-handed, bringing the ball almost behind his head before releasing.

Luisetti went on to become a star player at Stanford University, where he popularized the shot during the late 1930s.

Joe Fulks, a player at Murray State, took the concept a step further. He took his shot on the run, spinning away from the defender and often switching hands before firing his shot. Fulks' unorthodox approach made him one of the top scorers in pro basketball after World War II, a record highlighted by a 63-point game.

Hank Luisetti once scored 50 points in a college game.

Bobby McDermott used the two-handed set shot to become the most prolific scorer of the 1930s and '40s.

TWO HANDS AT ALL TIMES

The two-handed set shot used to be the only shot in the game. Coaches wouldn't let players try it any other way—and there was something to be said for it. The shot was highly accurate: Barney Sedran used it to make 17 shots in a 1914 game, all of them from 25 feet or more. Later, Rick Barry used a variation to shoot his free throws for a time during the 1970s.

But maybe the best two-handed set shooter was Bobby McDermott, who played professionally from 1935 to 1950. He led three different leagues in scoring while leading several different teams to championships. The 5-11 McDermott could score from anywhere on the court, earning the nickname "Mr. Inside and Mr. Outside."

In 1946, National Basketball League coaches voted McDermott the best player in the history of the game. He would be the last great two-handed set shooter, though, because once defenders started jumping, the shot became too easy to block.

One of the NBA's best jump shots belongs to the Sacramento Kings' Peja Stojakovic, who displays classic form here.

FROM WAY DOWNTOWN

The three-point shot has been in the NBA for about 25 years. But the concept—that shots of a certain length should be worth more than two points—was first put into practice by the American Basketball League (ABL) in 1961. The ABL lasted less than two seasons but the three-point shot proved to have more staying power than the league's.

The American Basketball Association (ABA) used a three-pointer throughout its nine seasons (1967–1976) and, three years after the ABA's demise, the NBA joined the bandwagon and finally adopted the shot.

The benefits of a three-pointer include more space in the middle of the court, more opportunities for shorter players, and more comebacks and fantastic finishes.

Reggie Miller knocks down another three-pointer. The Indiana Pacers guard has made more shots from beyond the arc than any other player in NBA history.

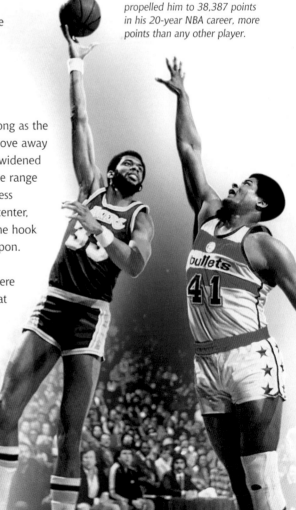

Kareem Abdul-Jabbar's sky-hook propelled him to 38,387 points in his 20-year NBA career, more points than any other player.

THE DOCTOR IS IN

Dunks began to gain acceptance during the early 1970s, but Julius Erving elevated the slam dunk to an art form. Dr. J electrified crowds with his ballhandling and his

Long before everyone wanted to be like Mike, they wanted to be Dr. J, who redefined the game with his airborne artistry.

ability to score from anywhere, but most of all he did it by staying airborne for what seemed like an eternity during his dunks, which often defied belief and inspired a generation of players.

As Michael Jordan said, "I would never have had the visions I had if I hadn't seen Dr. J in his prime."

HEAVEN SENT

The hook shot has been around as long as the NBA. When George Mikan had to move away from the basket because the league widened the foul lane, he simply extended the range on his hook shot, and it proved no less effective. But it was another Lakers center, Kareem Abdul-Jabbar, who turned the hook shot into the ultimate offensive weapon.

He began shooting hooks in the fourth grade, but it was at UCLA where he perfected the high-arcing shot that seemed to come from above— hence the name "sky-hook." Kareem, his 7-2 frame fully extended, sent his shot at the highest point, over everyone, even other 7-footers.

As he reflected later, "I knew I could get it off whenever I wanted."

Changing the Game

BASKETBALL HAS PROVEN remarkably adaptable, a sport that has embraced change rather than resist the inevitable. If games are too slow, use a shot clock to speed things up. If a player wants to try something new, let him have a little fun. Experimentation and individual expression have always been a part of basketball. That's how the seemingly mundane act of passing the ball became an art form in the hands of Bob Cousy. Conventional wisdom held that someone who stood 6 feet 9 inches could not play point guard. But along came Magic Johnson, a player of such immense talent that the old rules no longer applied. Like the players on the floor, the sport of basketball is in constant motion, as illustrated here.

THE ART OF THE PASS

Scorers get most of the attention, but often the most creative players are the ones distributing the ball. The first star of this type was Bob Davies during the late 1940s. The Rochester Royals' guard dazzled fans, teammates, and opponents alike with his ballhandling.

Davies was followed by the Celtics' Bob Cousy (pictured in action above), whose behind-the-back dribbling and no-look passes earned him the nickname "Houdini of the Hardwood." Teammates learned never to take their eye off the ball, even if Cousy did.

Pete Maravich's teammates followed that rule too. Maravich, a prolific scorer in college and the pros, was also a great passer and ballhandler who could deliver the ball through the smallest seam on the court.

"Pistol" Pete Maravich was a one-man offensive show throughout the 1970s.

George Mikan (#99) so dominated the game that the NBA widened the foul lane in 1951. But thanks to hook shots like the one pictured above, Mikan still led the Lakers to multiple titles in the '50s.

IN THE NICK OF TIME

Behind 6-10 George Mikan, the Minneapolis Lakers were unbeatable on the floor. In response, the NBA remade the floor, widening the foul lane from six feet to twelve in 1951, to prevent Mikan (and other big men) from camping out under the hoop. It also opened up the court.

But teams still held on to the ball for long periods of time, which forced opponents to foul, resulting in dull games. The solution? A shot clock. In 1954, the NBA adopted Syracuse owner Danny Biasone's proposal that each team be given 24 seconds to shoot before losing the ball to the other team.

The league also limited teams to six fouls per quarter, after which their opponents received free throws. These new rules transformed basketball into an exciting, fast-paced, athletic display.

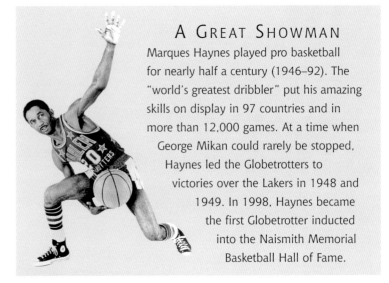

A GREAT SHOWMAN

Marques Haynes played pro basketball for nearly half a century (1946–92). The "world's greatest dribbler" put his amazing skills on display in 97 countries and in more than 12,000 games. At a time when George Mikan could rarely be stopped, Haynes led the Globetrotters to victories over the Lakers in 1948 and 1949. In 1998, Haynes became the first Globetrotter inducted into the Naismith Memorial Basketball Hall of Fame.

OFF AND RUNNING

During the mid-1950s, Red Auerbach's Boston Celtics were an entertaining team that ran the floor and scored a lot of points. Of course, they also gave up a lot of points, which is why the NBA title proved elusive—at least until Bill Russell arrived in 1957.

Centers were supposed to score, but Auerbach asked Russell to concentrate on defense and rebounding. So Russell cleared the glass, swatted away shots in the paint, and fired outlet passes. The Celtics' fast break was better than ever because the guards were immediately off and running with the shot, knowing Russell had the defensive end covered. Using this formula, Russell led Boston to 11 NBA titles in 13 seasons, the greatest dynasty in professional team sports and the most championships for any individual athlete.

Bill Russell's (right) defense sparked the Boston Celtics' fast break—and spurred them to 11 NBA titles.

BIG GUARDS AND FAST CENTERS

A player's position used to speak volumes. Centers stayed near the hoop, forwards rebounded and played tough defense, and guards handled the ball and shot from the outside. Today, centers can be found leading the break and shooting three-pointers, and forwards and guards can be found everywhere.

The evolution began with Oscar Robertson during the 1960s. The 6-5 guard scored, rebounded, and handled the ball while playing rugged defense. The Big O did not specialize—he simply did everything well.

The progression continued with the arrival of Earvin "Magic" Johnson in 1979. Magic could play anywhere on the floor, but it was at point guard—at 6-9, he is the tallest ever at that position—where Johnson made history. Never had there been a guard who could score inside and out, rebound, post up, and distribute the ball like he did. He routinely delivered spectacular passes that left defenders shaking their heads. And Magic so obviously enjoyed himself that dishing the ball became cool.

Currently, Kevin Garnett, who stands 6 feet 11 inches, is just as likely to knock down a 20-footer as he is to post up. KG is too quick for big men, and much too tall for smaller players. Power forward, small forward, center, even point guard—Garnett has played every spot.

Magic Johnson averaged an NBA record 11.2 assists per game during his 13-season career.

Though he stands 6-11, Kevin Garnett often can be found leading—and finishing—fast breaks.

Clothing and Equipment

BASKETBALL HAS CERTAINLY COME A LONG WAY from its state in the 1890s, when the ball had to be retrieved after every goal. Alterations in equipment and clothing have been both causes and results of changes in the way the game is played. Many brands of basketball-specific clothing are fashionable in and of themselves, and drastic modifications to the sport's rules, like the addition of the 24-second shot clock in 1954, have often made an immediate impact. Yet despite all the numerous changes, basketball has remained basically the same game over the years.

Through technology and mass production, basketball sneakers have gotten more practical and comfortable over the years. From the bottom: leather shoes of the early 1900s eventually gave way to the revolutionary Nike Air Jordan sneaker in the mid-1980s, which then paved the way for fancier engineered footwear like the ultra-modern Reebok NBA Denial shoe.

EVOLUTION OF CLOTHING

One of the primary reasons basketball is such an inclusive sport for people of all backgrounds is the simplicity of the uniform. From the game's earliest days, all a player has needed to show up with is a shirt, some shorts, and a pair of shoes.

Over the years, a professional (male) basketball uniform has not changed much, still consisting of a tank-top jersey, shorts, and shoes (often high-tops to preserve the ankle joints).

With the immense popularity of the NBA and WNBA, and their players and teams, each item of the uniform has become a fashion statement on its own, even far away from the court.

It's been quite a dramatic shift for the uniforms worn by female basketball players over time. Social change and practicality took them from wearing essentially full-length robes (far left) to high-tech and streamlined designs nearly identical to male players, as demonstrated at left by Diana Taurasi of the Phoenix Mercury.

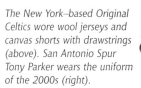

The New York–based Original Celtics wore wool jerseys and canvas shorts with drawstrings (above). San Antonio Spur Tony Parker wears the uniform of the 2000s (right).

EVOLUTION OF EQUIPMENT

In 1891, basket goals were nothing more than peach baskets with small holes punched through the bottom, raised 10 feet above the ground. But game equipment soon evolved to a wire-frame rim that featured a trap-door attached to a string as a ball return.

Wooden backboards were replaced by smaller ones made of plexiglass in the 1940s, before larger glass ones were phased in. Backboards now measure 42 by 72 inches, while the rim is always 18 inches in diameter.

Basketballs have evolved as well, although not as much: they have always been made of leather and maintain 9-inch diameters and circumferences of just under 30 inches.

Raised peach baskets (right) soon gave way to backboards that featured wire-frame rims and an innovative ball return (above).

24-SECOND SHOT CLOCK

In 1954, Syracuse Nationals owner Danny Biasone figured that the average game contained about 120 shots between the two teams, meaning that teams averaged about one shot every 24 seconds in a 48-minute game. Forcing shots before the 24 seconds expired would lead to an increase in scoring—and thus game attendence.

Modern technology has allowed for baskets with heavy glass backboards, complete with protective padding, shot clocks, and cameras, all held in place by well over a ton of support structure.

Since the game is now played less on the floor, there is no longer a need for all players to wear the knee pads of the 1920s (above). But knee braces are still necessities for some players (right).

Panel-style basketballs (above) dominated the game's early days before giving way to lace-up balls (middle) that lasted from 1894 to the 1940s, and ultimately the modern-day ball (far right), which contains an inflatable bladder made from rubber and nylon string. The exterior of all three models are made from various types of leather.

Coaches: The Top 10 in NBA History

THEY ARE TEACHERS, strategists, motivators, communicators, and most importantly, winners. They set the agenda for their teams and are judged by the end result. A pressure-filled position that is demanding yet rewarding, coaching can be done with differing styles and often amount to an artform. At the professional level, coaching requires a special talent to endure the ups and downs of a long season. Although there have been numerous great coaches who have roamed the sidelines throughout the league's nearly 60-year history, the men on the following four pages were named the Top 10 Coaches in NBA History as part of the "NBA at 50" celebration during the 1996–97 season.

◄ Red Auerbach

His record is staggering: nine championships for the Boston Celtics in 10 years, including an amazing eight in a row and more than 1,000 combined regular-season and playoff wins (1,037). Yet the true genius of Red Auerbach goes beyond the statistics. Not only was Auerbach the ultimate motivator, consistently tapping into his player's strengths, but he was also a great talent evaluator. Auerbach, the general manager, acquired some of the NBA's greatest players (Bill Russell, Tom Heinsohn, and K. C. Jones among others) for Auerbach, the coach, resulting in the NBA's greatest dynasty.

▲ Chuck Daly

Thirty-six years of inconsistency vanished for the Pistons when Chuck Daly arrived in Detroit, cultivating a reputation as the ultimate player's coach while also implementing a physical, intimidating style of defense. The approach paid off as the Pistons won back-to-back titles in 1989 and '90, and captured three division titles in eight seasons. Daly also earned acclaim for coaching the Dream Team to the Olympic gold medal in 1992.

▶ Red Holzman

His philosophy was simple and straightforward: "If you play good hard defense, the offense will take care of itself." Sure enough, the New York Knicks heeded the words of their coach Red Holzman to championship perfection. Under Holzman, the Knicks won two NBA titles in three seasons in the 1970s, thanks to a pressing, defensive-oriented style of play that accentuated the talents of future Hall of Famers Clyde Frazier, Willis Reed, Dave DeBusschere, and Bill Bradley. Holzman spent 18 seasons as a head coach, 14 with the Knicks, and amassed 696 victories.

▲ Bill Fitch

Bill Fitch's reward for a successful 12-year college coaching career was earning a shot with the expansion Cleveland Cavaliers in 1970. He certainly made the most of that opportunity, leading the Cavs for nine seasons, including a storybook 1976 Eastern Conference Finals run versus the mighty Boston Celtics. Fitch eventually landed in Boston in 1979–80, the same season as Larry Bird, and the Celtics won the championship the next year. Fitch also coached the Houston Rockets, New Jersey Nets, and Los Angeles Clippers on his way to 944 career wins.

◀ Phil Jackson

A disciple of Bill Fitch, his college coach at North Dakota, and legendary Knicks coach Red Holzman, Phil Jackson certainly learned from some of the greatest basketball minds around, and he put the knowledge to good use as head coach of the Chicago Bulls. In nine seasons, Jackson and the Bulls won six NBA titles and six division titles. Jackson continued his championship streak when he took over the Los Angeles Lakers, leading them to three consecutive titles in his first three seasons. His total is nine championships in his first 12 years as head coach.

THE NBA'S FIRST DYNASTY

John Kundla became head coach of the Minneapolis Lakers in 1947, at the tender age of 31, and quickly set the standard for coaching excellence during the NBA's infancy, leading the Lakers to five titles in six years from 1948–49 through 1953–54. He was the first coach ever to win three NBA titles in a row, and he coached six Hall of Famers, including the NBA's first superstar, George Mikan. In 11 NBA seasons, the low-key Kundla compiled a 423-302 record for a .583 winning percentage.

◄ Don Nelson

Creative, unconventional, and innovative are just some of the characteristics that have served Don Nelson well in his 26 years (and counting) of coaching in the NBA. Only one other coach in NBA history—Lenny Wilkens—has notched more victories (1,268) than Nellie. The three-time NBA Coach of the Year is a master when it comes to taking advantage of matchups and implementing new strategies that routinely place opponents on their heels. Nelson has enjoyed long and successful runs with the Bucks and Warriors, and is currently coaching the Mavericks.

◀ Pat Riley

In Los Angeles, Pat Riley established himself as one of the NBA's greatest coaches by leading the Lakers to four titles in nine seasons during the '80s. After moving to New York, he cemented his place among the all-time greats when he led the Knicks to their first NBA Finals appearance in 21 years. In Miami, Riley transformed the Heat into contenders, routinely going for the Eastern Conference title. Not only did Riley win with different coaching styles, but he looked good doing it, pacing up and down the court in his custom Armani suits.

▶ Jack Ramsay

In 20-plus seasons, Jack Ramsay successfully guided four different franchises and compiled 864 wins for his career. The crowning achievement on Ramsay's blustery résumé was the Portland Trail Blazers' improbable run to the championship, upsetting the heavily favored Philadelphia 76ers in six games during the 1977 NBA Finals. Ramsay was inducted in the Hall of Fame in 1992.

▲ Lenny Wilkens

In 1968, Lenny Wilkens was named player-coach of the Seattle SuperSonics, becoming only the second African-American in NBA history to be appointed head coach. Twenty-six years later, Wilkens became the league's all-time winningest coach, surpassing Red Auerbach. Success wasn't anything new to Wilkens, who as a player with the Hawks, Sonics, and Cavaliers, participated in nine NBA All-Star Games. Wilkens reached his first coaching pinnacle when he guided the Sonics to the 1979 NBA title. He has amassed over 1,300 wins so far in his career.

Coaches: Two or More NBA Championships

HANNUM. RUSSELL. HEINSOHN. TOMJANOVICH. POPOVICH. What do these men all have in common? They are among an exclusive group of NBA coaches who have won two or more championships. This exclusive fraternity doesn't admit just anyone. Its requirements are stringent: multiple championships. Only 12 coaches in the history of the NBA have been admitted to this club, with Gregg Popovich being its most recent member in 2003.

▲ Alex Hannum

Alex Hannum was professional basketball's ultimate Mr. Fix-it. The former NBA player turned three franchises—the Syracuse Nationals, the San Francisco Warriors, and the Oakland Oaks of the ABA—into winners. He also became the first professional coach to win an NBA title (St. Louis Hawks in 1957 and Philadelphia 76ers in '67) and an ABA title (Oakland Oaks in '69).

Tom Heinsohn ▶

An important contributor to the Celtics' dynasty as a player, Tom Heinsohn was asked to keep the championship express going as head coach after Bill Russell retired in 1969. He fulfilled the request by leading the Celtics to five consecutive division titles and two NBA Finals titles in nine seasons. Heinsohn was NBA Coach of the Year for the 1972–73 season.

▶ Gregg Popovich

The NBA coaching elite officially welcomed its newest member when the San Antonio Spurs won the 2003 NBA title under the leadership of Gregg Popovich. The former coach of Pomona-Pitzer, a Division III school, Popovich led the Spurs to the franchise's first NBA championship in 1999. The Air Force Academy graduate became the ninth fastest coach in NBA history to reach 300 wins by surpassing that milestone in the second half of the 2002–03 season.

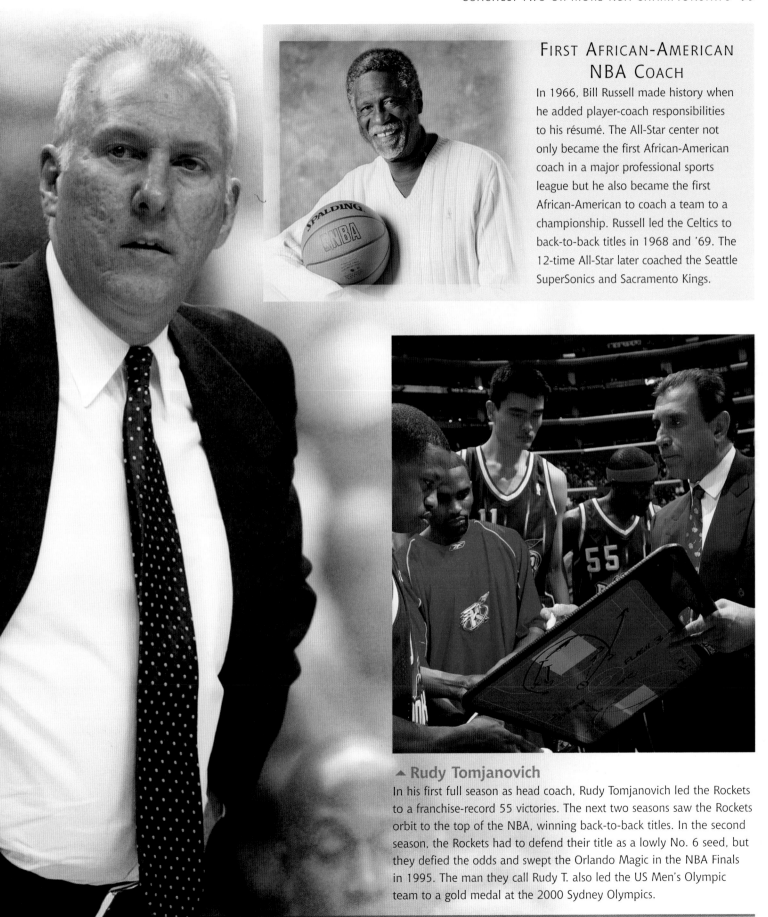

FIRST AFRICAN-AMERICAN NBA COACH

In 1966, Bill Russell made history when he added player-coach responsibilities to his résumé. The All-Star center not only became the first African-American coach in a major professional sports league but he also became the first African-American to coach a team to a championship. Russell led the Celtics to back-to-back titles in 1968 and '69. The 12-time All-Star later coached the Seattle SuperSonics and Sacramento Kings.

▲ Rudy Tomjanovich

In his first full season as head coach, Rudy Tomjanovich led the Rockets to a franchise-record 55 victories. The next two seasons saw the Rockets orbit to the top of the NBA, winning back-to-back titles. In the second season, the Rockets had to defend their title as a lowly No. 6 seed, but they defied the odds and swept the Orlando Magic in the NBA Finals in 1995. The man they call Rudy T. also led the US Men's Olympic team to a gold medal at the 2000 Sydney Olympics.

Coaches: 500 or More Wins

ANOTHER PATH TO NBA COACHING SUCCESS is via the college route. Coaches such as Larry Brown, Cotton Fitzsimmons, and Del Harris are just a few of the men who have established themselves at the collegiate level before succeeding in the NBA. Brown, who won multiple Coach of the Year awards in the American Basketball Association, coached UCLA for two seasons before moving on to Kansas, where he led the Jayhawks to the 1988 NCAA title. Coaching in college isn't all that these coaches have in common though. These men, along with others profiled on the next four pages, are all members of the exclusive 500-win club.

◄ Rick Adelman

During 1990–91, only his second season in the Rose City, Rick Adelman led the Portland Trail Blazers to the NBA Finals against the Detroit Pistons. He followed up with yet another appearance two years later against the Chicago Bulls. Then, after spending two seasons coaching the Golden State Warriors, Adelman took over the reins in Sacramento and eventually surpassed the 600-win plateau during the 2002–03 season. He has coached his teams to 12 playoff appearances in his first 14 seasons.

▲ Al Attles

The greatest upset in NBA Finals history was the handiwork of Golden State Warrior head coach Al Attles. The 1975 NBA Finals featured Golden State, owners of a 48-34 record, versus the Washington Bullets, who boasted the NBA's best record that season at 60-22. Warrior Rick Barry starred in the series, taking home MVP honors as Golden State's depth proved to be too much for the Bullets, who were defeated in a shocking four-game sweep. Attles went on to win 557 victories in 14 seasons with the Warriors.

COACHED SEVEN DIFFERENT NBA PLAYOFF TEAMS

Everywhere Larry Brown, a former ABA player, has coached he has been a success: Denver, New Jersey, San Antonio, Los Angeles (Clippers), Indiana, Philadelphia, and now Detroit. He has led his teams to six division titles, accumulated more than 900 wins, and has made two NBA Finals appearances. The 2001 NBA Coach of the Year also coached four seasons in the ABA and seven in college, leading the University of Kansas to the 1988 NCAA title.

◀ Mike Fratello

In his 13 seasons as a head coach, Mike Fratello has led his teams to the playoffs nine times. He enjoyed a great run in Atlanta, where in seven-plus seasons he led the Hawks to four consecutive seasons of 50 or more victories and five postseason appearances. The 1986 NBA Coach of the Year then moved to Cleveland, where he led the Cavaliers to four postseason berths in six seasons. Fratello has compiled 572 wins.

▲ Del Harris

After spending nine seasons as the head coach at Earlham College (Indiana) and five as an assistant in the ABA, Del Harris was more than ready for his first head-coaching opportunity. In only his second season in Houston, Harris led the 40-42 Rockets all the way to the 1981 NBA Finals, where they fell to the Celtics in six games. It was only the third time in NBA history that a team with a sub .500 record advanced to basketball's biggest stage. In his 13-year, head-coaching career, which has also included stops in Milwaukee and Los Angeles, Harris has compiled a 556-457 record.

▲ Cotton Fitzsimmons

Cotton Fitzsimmons had a 21-year career that began and ended in Phoenix. There were other successful stops along the way—four seasons in Atlanta, one in Buffalo, six in Kansas City, two in San Antonio—but regardless of what team he was coaching, one thing was certain: Fitzsimmons' teams always came ready to play. The two-time NBA Coach of the Year won 832 games during his career.

▲ K. C. Jones

As a Hall of Fame player for the Boston Celtics, K. C. Jones knew all about championship success. After all, he was a member of eight NBA title teams. The former University of San Francisco standout also achieved the ultimate success as a coach, guiding the Celtics to two titles in a three-year span during the 1980s, and four NBA Finals appearances in a four-year period. Jones began his coaching career with the Capital Bullets and led them to the 1975 Finals in only his second season at the helm. He also coached the Seattle SuperSonics in the early '90s.

John MacLeod ▶

His numbers are impressive— 707 victories in 20 NBA seasons, 14 of which were spent in the Valley of the Sun. John MacLeod guided the Phoenix Suns to five Western Conference finishes, including one memorable Cinderella run that included what some consider the greatest game in NBA history: the Game 5 triple-overtime thriller of the 1976 NBA Finals. The 42-40 Suns lost that classic to the Celtics, and eventually the series, but not before giving their fans a ride they would never forget.

▶ George Karl

His coaching career began in the CBA, which eventually led him to head-coaching stops in Cleveland and Golden State over the next four years. After coaching overseas in Spain and returning to the CBA, Karl eventually landed in Seattle in 1991. Over the course of the next seven years, he finally found his footing as a head coach, leading the Sonics to four division titles and one NBA Finals appearance. Karl also worked his magic in Milwaukee, leading the Bucks to their first playoff appearance in seven years.

▶ Doug Moe

Doug Moe left an indelible mark, on and off the court. A reporter's dream, he routinely provided colorful and glib quotes, and players loved his up-tempo system. In 10 seasons in Denver, Moe compiled a 432-357 (.548) record and led the Nuggets to the postseason nine times in a row. The Nuggets' high-octane offense led the NBA in scoring during six of Moe's 10 seasons at the helm, while establishing the league's all-time, single-season record of 126.5 points per game in 1981–82.

▲ Jerry Sloan

For nearly 20 years, Jerry Sloan has led the Utah Jazz to great success — six division titles, two NBA Finals appearances, and 16 trips to the postseason. After the 2000–01 season, Sloan became only the third coach in NBA history (behind Pat Riley and Phil Jackson) to win at least 50 games in 10 seasons. An intense, hard-nosed player who once starred for the Chicago Bulls in the late 1960s and '70s, Sloan has adopted that same no-retreat, no-surrender philosophy with great results as a head coach.

◀ Dick Motta

In a head-coaching career that spanned 25 years, Dick Motta certainly left an enduring mark on the NBA. In his eight seasons in Chicago, the Bulls ranked among the NBA's best defensive teams, earning playoff berths in six seasons. Motta then moved on to Washington, where he coached Wes Unseld, Elvin Hayes, and the Bullets to back-to-back NBA Finals appearances, netting a championship in 1978. Two years later, Motta led the expansion Dallas Mavericks to four playoff appearances in their first seven seasons. Motta, who also coached Sacramento for three seasons before returning to Dallas for three more, owns 935 career wins.

▲ Gene Shue

As a player, Gene Shue enjoyed great success, earning All-Star honors during five of his 10 NBA seasons. His career as an NBA head coach wasn't any different. In 22 seasons, Shue coached five different teams and twice earned NBA Coach of the Year honors. Shue reached basketball's ultimate stage when he led the Philadelphia 76ers to the NBA Finals in 1997.

Rules of the Game

A SPORT IS NOT A SPORT without rules, and most of basketball's rules were not made to be broken—the game has never allowed for such things as running with the ball, a seventh personal foul, or a four-point basket. But there have been notable changes to the rule book over time. In addition to the introduction of the 24-second shot clock in 1954, several other rules changes have been adopted over the years, some even in direct response to the dominance of a few individual players, such as George Mikan, Wilt Chamberlain, and Charles Barkley.

Official scorers keep track of everything: points, rebounds, assists, turnovers, fouls, you name it. They also play a valuable role in assisting referees throughout a game.

THE ORIGINAL RULES

Dr. James Naismith knew that the young men in his YMCA gym needed guidelines if his new game stood any chance of fulfilling his goal of popularizing an indoor non-violent game. The rules have been modified over time but the principles have remained constant.

Here are some that stood the test of time: "The ball may be thrown in any direction with one or both hands" (except when backcourt violations have been committed).

"The ball may be batted in any direction with one or both hands" (this led to the evolution of the blocked shot).

"A player cannot run with the ball, the player must throw it from the spot on which he catches it, with allowance to be made for a man who catches the ball when running at a good speed" (a player must dribble or pass).

"No shouldering, holding, pushing, tripping, or striking in any way the person of an opponent shall be allowed" (these result in fouls or ejections).

And, of course, "The side making the most goals in regulation shall be declared the winner."

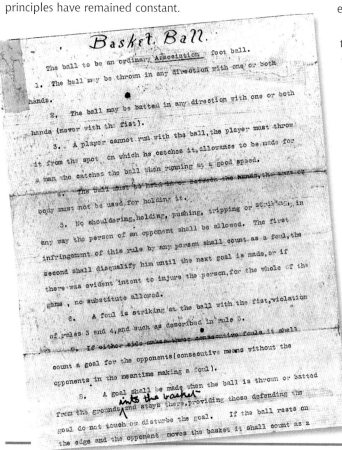

Many of the original 13 rules of the game, as first issued by Dr. James Naismith in 1891, have stayed the same for more than a century.

THE NBA RULES

Every season, the NBA prints a rule guide over 50 pages in length that touches on every conceivable rule definition, foul, equipment specification, and rare exception. Many rules are seldom, if ever, necessary, such as: "A team must have five players on the floor at all times. If a team has no available substitutes and a player receive his sixth foul, rather than fouling out, he must remain on the floor and his team is assessed a technical, a personal, and a team foul."

Rules also govern players' uniforms: "Each number must be not less than 3/4 inches in width and not less than 6 inches in height on both the front and the back of the jersey. Each player shall have his surname affixed to the back of his game jersey in letters at least 2 inches in height."

GEORGE MIKAN

George Mikan blocked so many shots as a collegiate player that the NCAA introduced a rule outlawing goaltending—when a defensive player blocks a shot while it is on the downward side of its path to the basket.

Yet the 6-10 center still managed to take his dominance into the NBA, where the league doubled the width of the foul lanes (from 6 feet to 12 feet) in an attempt to level the playing field for his opponents. It actually made him better all-around, as Mikan added a jump shot to his repertoire. It also enabled his teammates to cut to the basket, adding balance to an already unbeatable team.

George Mikan (right) of the Minneapolis Lakers was an offensive and defensive force.

WILT CHAMBERLAIN

Wilt Chamberlain is credited with single-handedly causing several rule changes, such as widening the foul lanes (from 12 feet to 16 feet), instituting offensive goaltending, and a revision of the rules governing inbounding the ball and shooting free throws.

At one point in his career, the 7-1 Chamberlain would "take" free throws by leaping from behind the foul line with the ball to deposit it in the basket.

Wilt Chamberlain followed in Mikan's footsteps as a big man who could do it all, and the league was compelled to do something after he performed such unprecented feats as scoring 100 points in a single game.

One of the game's outstanding forwards of the 1980s and '90s, Charles Barkley would take his time after receiving the ball in the low post, to the point where the league set a five-second time limit on backing in with the ball.

FIVE-SECOND BACK-TO-THE-BASKET

A new rule was insititued in 1999 to avoid lengthy individual possessions. Before this, when a player received the ball in the low post with his back facing the basket, he would often slowly back in his defender before eventually pivoting for the shot, trying to get as close to the rim as possible.

The entire process was lengthy, and so recurrent that a new rule was introduced giving players five seconds from the time they receive a pass to turn and face the basket for a shot before having to give up possession.

The Top Misunderstood NBA Rules

WHAT IS CONSIDERED A CHARGE and what is considered a block? Was that goaltending or a clean block? In NBA basketball, there is never an easy answer because of the fast-paced action that takes place for 48 minutes. Decisions are made in a split second by referees. Some rules are easy to follow, such as traveling or stepping out of bounds, while others, such as an illegal pick, aren't so easy to identify when watching a game. So, to help ensure full enjoyment and to reduce any potential confusion, here is a list of the most misunderstood rules in the game of NBA basketball (rules differ for WNBA, FIBA, and NCAA).

TRAVELING

To start a dribble, a player must release the ball from his hand before his pivot foot leaves the floor or he has committed a traveling violation. A player is allowed a one-two count after gathering the ball while attempting a lay-up or running shot. Many people think a player travels when he covers a long distance but an agile 7-0 player can go a long way in just a one-two count rhythm. If a player jumps in the air, he must shoot or pass, he can't start a dribble or land with the ball.

BLOCKS/CHARGES

A block/charge foul occurs when a defender tries to get in front of his man to stop him from going in that direction. If he doesn't get into a legal defensive position and contact occurs, it's a blocking foul. If he gets to a legal position and the offensive player runs into him it's a charging foul. In both situations, if the contact is minimal, the foul may not be called.

To get into a legal position against the dribbler, the defender just needs to get in front of him. On a drive to the basket, the defender must get to his position before the shooter starts his upward shooting motion. In most other cases, the defender must get into position and allow enough distance for the offensive player to stop and/or change direction.

TECHNICAL FOULS

While certain behavior is considered worthy of penalization by some officials and not others, all officials are trained on decision-making standards that are expected to be applied consistently. Nevertheless, individual officials are expected to control the game at their own discretion. When they do call a technical foul, one free throw is attempted by any player on the fouled team in the game.

A penalty separate of technical fouls is the accumulation of team fouls. Each team is allowed four team fouls in each period. On the fifth foul and every one that follows, the player fouled receives two free-throw attempts if he wasn't in the act of shooting. During overtimes, he shoots on the fourth team foul and each one that follows.

ILLEGAL PICKS

A pick is when an offensive player gets to a legal position on the court in the path of a defender for the purpose of slowing him down or making him change direction. An illegal pick is when the defender does not get into a legal position.

When picking a stationary opponent from the back, you must give that player a step to stop and/or change direction since he can't see you. If he's standing still you can stand right next to him as long as you are clearly in his sight.

If the opponent is moving, you must get to your position and give him enough distance to stop and/or change direction. The speed of the player will determine the distance required. You can't just jump in front of a player at the last second.

Is this the result of a charge or a block? It might not be either if there wasn't any contact between the Denver Nuggets' Nené (defending) and the Portland Trail Blazers' Theo Ratliff (shooting).

FLAGRANT FOULS

There are two types of flagrant fouls. Flagrant foul No. 1 is unnecessary contact, usually when a defensive player swings and makes hard contact with the offensive player or makes hard contact and then follows through.

Flagrant foul No. 2 is unnecessary and excessive contact, usually with a swinging motion, hard contact, and a follow through.

Both fouls carry a penalty of two free throws and the fouled team retains possession. A player is ejected on two No.1s or one No. 2.

CLEAR PATH TO THE BASKET

If a fast break starts in a team's backcourt and a defender fouls any offensive player when the team is going to score an easy basket, a clear-path foul has occurred.

The foul only happens if there isn't a defender ahead of the ball, where he could defend against the easy basket.

HAND CHECKING

A defender can't place and keep his hand on an opponent unless he's in the area near the basket and is not facing it. A defender can momentarily touch an opponent with his hand anywhere on the court as long as it does not affect his movement (speed, quickness, balance, or rhythm).

SUBSTITUTIONS

During a full timeout, all players can be substituted. During a 20-second timeout, only one player can be replaced by the calling team and one by the other team, but if the calling team doesn't replace a player, the opponent can't either. All players can be replaced if the 20-second timeout is called in the last two minutes of the fourth period or the last two minutes of an overtime.

Once a player enters the game, he must remain until the ball is legally touched or a foul, change of possession, or administration of the blood rule is committed.

GOALTENDING

When a player shoots the ball, a defender can't touch it after it reaches its highest point or the shot is ruled successful. A defender also can't touch a shot after it has touched the backboard and is going towards the rim, even if it's going up. Once the ball is on or directly above the rim, a defender can't touch the ball. If the ball is rolling on top of the rim, a defender can't touch the ball or the rim.

If an offensive player touches the ball in any of the above instances, basket interference is ruled and no points can be scored.

Once the ball rolls to the outside of the rim, the shot is over and any player on either team can touch the ball.

DEFENSIVE THREE SECONDS

A defensive player is not allowed inside the key area for more than 3 seconds unless he is guarding the player with the ball or is actively guarding any opponent.

To be considered actively guarding, a defender must be within an arm's length of an offensive player as they both move through the key. He can't just stand there and put his arms out to receive a new three-second count.

Did Carlos Boozer (#1) block this shot by Bobby Jackson? Or is he goaltending? The answer depends on whether the ball is on the way up or on the way down.

NBA Referees

EVEN AS THE GAME OF BASKETBALL has rapidly developed over the past 110 years, the area of officiating has stayed constant as referees have continued to apply the rules as they see fit. In recent years, the stakes have become higher for professional teams, and officiating is adjusting. While technology allows for instant replay (in selective situations), official hand signals and referee/player communication have remained uniform over the years. Although referees are relatively anonymous, Pat Kennedy, Earl Strom, and Violet Palmer have stood out.

Officials gather at the scorers' table to review a video replay, something that is only done for shots and foul calls occurring as time expires at the ends of periods.

INSTANT REPLAY

After the 2001–02 season, the NBA decided to allow the use of instant video replay for the use of reviewing shots and foul calls occurring as time expired at the ends of periods. Shots are most often reviewed on whether they had left the shooter's hand before the period buzzer sounded, or were shot from behind the three-point line or from out-of-bounds.

The final call is made after the officiating crew has gathered as much information as possible, and a review has been made. The original call can only be reversed if the crew agrees that there is "clear and conclusive" visual evidence to do so.

REFEREE/PLAYER COMMUNICATION

Officials must meet with team captains before the start of every game to clarify any questions they might have regarding the ensuing contest. Refs should also be aware of any controversies that may affect a team's behavior.

During the course of an NBA game, it's not unusual to see players interacting with officials, and not necessarily in an adversarial fashion. Players are allowed to ask why a foul was called, or for clarification of any other call.

REFEREE SIGNALS

In a noisy NBA arena, with fans, music, and other things making it too loud to hear at most times, officials have stuck to a set of hand signals for marking made shots, fouls, time-outs, and other stoppages of play.

In addition to those shown to the right, separate hand signals exist for: basket interference, blocking, canceling score or play, charging, designating an offender, double fouls, illegal screens out of bounds, jump balls, pushing, technical fouls, three-second violations, traveling, 24-second shot clock violations, and 20-second timeouts.

So when fans can't hear the public-address system, the old-fashioned hand signals can tell them what is going on.

Goaltending
flag from wrist

Illegal Dribble
patting motion
call team colour

Direction of Play
point direction
call team colour

Time-in
chop hand to side

Time-out
open palm

Personal Foul
clenched fist

Holding
signal foul:
grasp wrist

Loose Ball Foul
extended arms to shoulder

**Illegal use
of Hands** signal
foul: strike wrist

GAME-DAY OPERATIONS OF AN NBA REFEREE

On game day, officials meet to go over game reports, game summaries, and specific cases from previous games between the two teams slotted to play that night. They break down video and analyze the case studies as they prepare for the matchup.

During a game, referees are able to review calls during halftime to ensure accuracy.

Postgame, the officials review video from their game and perform an in-depth self-evaluation of their calls. Refs are also required to submit video breakdowns to the league via their private website, explaining their rulings in making calls. Refs are often scrutinized by administrators like the supervisor of officials and vice president of game operations.

NBA referee Violet Palmer works a 2004 NBA regular-season game in Salt Lake City, Utah.

VIOLET PALMER

On October 31, 1997, Violet Palmer made history by officiating the game between the Memphis Grizzlies and Dallas Mavericks—she became the first woman to referee a game for any all-male professional sports league.

A former starting point guard at Cal Poly-Pomona, where she was part of NCAA Division II championship teams in 1985 and '86, Palmer had plenty of officiating experience, mostly in women's collegiate games.

While the pace of men's basketball may be faster than women's, and the plays more focused above the rim, Palmer has said, "One thing we always have to remember is that basketball is basketball and that's where our training comes in."

After his retirement from on-court work, Pat Kennedy served as the NBA's Supervisor of Referees until 1950.

Thick-skinned and quick-witted, the late Earl Strom earned the respect of everyone he ever dealt with as an NBA referee.

PAT KENNEDY

One of the most colorful referees in basketball's early years, the late Matthew "Pat" Kennedy was a true showman at heart. His colorful nature left no doubt in players', coaches', and fans' minds which call he had made. But despite his animated style, Kennedy never lost control of a game.

He began officiating at age 20 in 1928. and worked nearly 4,000 games at high-school, college, and pro levels during the course of his illustrious career.

EARL STROM

Nicknamed "The Pied Piper" because of his unique ability to control the game with his whistle, Hall of Famer Earl Strom's reputation for fairness earned him the respect and admiration of players, coaches, and fans throughout his illustrious 32-year career.

Along with colleague Mendy Rudolph, Strom officiated the entire 1961 NBA Finals series that saw the Boston Celtics defeat the St. Louis Hawks in five games—the only time a series was worked by the same two refs.

Arenas

A LARGE PART OF THE EXPERIENCE of attending professional sporting events is the grandeur of the stadiums and arenas and their surrounding landscapes. A lot has changed since the days of old-fashioned arenas, which were practical, if not comfortable. Present-day arenas often represent the epitome of modern architecture, incorporating state-of-the-art design, economic demands (for luxury suites and the ability to host other events), and a desirable view from every seat. The exterior spaces of arenas have also proved to become a focal point of modern arena design, as tribute statues are growing in popularity.

The parquet hardwood floor from the original Boston Garden (above) was transferred to the FleetCenter in 1995 and lasted until December 1999, when it was replaced with a modern replica.

Toyota Center, the Houston Rockets' ultra-modern home, opened in 2003 in the heart of Houston, Texas.

THE EVOLUTION OF THE ARENA

Whether they are hosting sporting events, concerts, political conventions, or other expositions, arenas have come a long way over the years. Technology, economics, and modern demands have caused the design of arenas to evolve over time, from simple brick and stone boxes with raised centers, located in downtown areas, to whimsically curvy structures that can be placed in the heart of cities or nearby suburbs.

Even if not nearly as comfortable as their modern counterparts, classic arenas such as Chicago Stadium (above) and Boston Garden (right) certainly had charm.

Most arenas must have large outdoor spaces allotted to parking, as well as the space and ability to store and change the arena playing surface in a short period of time.

Many arenas feature outdoor gathering areas (for the beloved tailgating that fans live for during their teams' home games) and are located in the immediate vicinity of other sporting complexes. The Meadowlands complex in New Jersey has housed New Jersey Nets basketball, pro football, and harness horse racing virtually simultaneously.

Whether they are downtown or in the suburbs, one thing hasn't changed over the years—sports arenas can be the very epitome of the heart of a city.

The Boston Celtics had 16 championship banners and 19 retired numbers that hung in the rafters by the time the Boston Garden closed in 1995.

THE BOSTON GARDEN

One of the most hallowed grounds in all of professional sports history was the Boston Garden, which opened in 1928 and stood until its demolishment in 1997, two years after the new FleetCenter opened next door on Causeway Street. What the Garden lacked in amenities (some seats were literally behind column posts), it made up for in character and history. The NBA's Boston Celtics built one of the greatest dynasties there, winning 16 titles between 1957 and 1986.

For years, the Celtics were joined as tenants by the NHL's Boston Bruins, which explained the yellow-gold seats. Both the seat color-scheme and the distinctive parquet hardwood floor design made their way to the FleetCenter, which boasts no obstructed views. In 1995, the original parquet floor was transferred to the FleetCenter, and remained the team's playing surface until December 1999, when it was replaced with a modern replica. Most of the original floor was auctioned off by Sotheby's and sold to fans.

Michael Jordan is interviewed by Larry King at the unveiling of a bronze statue of Jordan outside the Chicago Bulls' new home, the United Center, in 1994.

Jerry West, NBA Commissioner David Stern, Magic and Cookie Johnson at the unveiling of Magic's statue.

PLAYER TRIBUTE STATUES

For the few athletes who have achieved immortality within their respective cities, one way to celebrate greatness close to home is by dedicating a tribute statue on arena grounds.

Michael Jordan was saluted by the Chicago Bulls with a 17-foot-high statue outside the United Center gates on November 1, 1994.

The statue quickly became one of Chicago's biggest tourist attractions.

Ten years later, retired Los Angeles Lakers great Magic Johnson was presented with a 17-foot-high bronze statue, depicting him leading a fast break, outside the Staples Center.

Behind the Scenes

A LOT HAS CHANGED since the game's earliest days, when Dr. James Naismith had to clear the gymnasium of gymnastics equipment in order to make open floor space for the game he invented for his students. From the moment modern-day NBA players arrive inside an arena on a game day, they have plenty of amenities at their disposal. Locker rooms are more comfortable then ever, while a trip to a staffed training room may prepare them better physically to be ready to compete. They even have their own TV and workout room, where they can watch previous games while using an exercise bike.

Benches, showers, hooks on the walls, and a laundry basket was about as fancy as a locker room (like the Boston Celtics' above) could get in the NBA's earlier days.

LOCKER ROOMS

NBA players and coaches are professionals and need sufficient facilities in which to spend their game days. Locker rooms, which started as nothing more than lockers and a bathing area, have evolved over the years to include meeting areas, training rooms, and video and equipment storage facilities.

At least when in their home arenas (locker rooms for visiting teams are much simpler), present-day players enjoy clean carpeted facilities that often include comfortable seating arrangements and even items for personal entertainment and nourishment, like televisions and dining areas. For many players, it's the next best thing to being in their own homes.

For home games, most NBA players provide their own transportation to and from their jobs, parking their automobiles in secure, reserved areas. Visiting teams generally take the team bus as a group to and from games, sometimes making two trips in a day (one for a morning shoot-around and another for the evening's game). Most players arrive at the arenas no earlier than three hours before tipoff, dressed either casually or in a tailored suit and tie.

Because many sportswriters and broadcast journalists must produce and file a game-night feature story before the tipoff of the game (on which they later file a separate story),

Dirk Nowitzki enters the locker room of the Dallas Mavericks. Like many pro locker rooms, the space serves as a kind of personal living room for the players.

many players and coaches make themselves available for media interviews near the locker rooms well before the start of games. This is a well-worn tradition that now exists in all professional sports leagues.

TRAINING ROOMS

There is more to players' preparations for games than just practicing. Training rooms, complete with professional trainers and strength-and-conditioning coaches on staff, are a mandatory stop for most players on game day, whether it be for a simple ankle taping, a muscle massage, or electronic stimulation. Not all treatments are therapeutic or rehabilitative though; many are just preventive and part of the normal maintenance of a professional athlete's body. Many teams also have weight-lifting and cardiological exercise areas on arena grounds or at the teams' practice facility.

The size and nature of a professional sports club requires teams to have a base of business, with both offices and a place for the team to practice. Some teams are able to utilize a single location for games, offices, and practices, such as the Indiana Pacers who work out of Conseco Fieldhouse all year long. Other clubs, like the New Jersey Nets have built

Dr. James Naismith first had to have gymnastics equipment cleared off the floor of the YMCA gymnasium in order to make way for the earliest basketball games. At least players could train easily before a game.

a separate facility near their home arena. The Nets' Champion Center opened in 1998, across town from their playing arena in East Rutherford, and features everything from two regulation courts, a player lounge, a current pool, a media room for journalists, and a team video room with theater seats.

Also included in most modern NBA arenas are fully functional video facilities, used for scouting purposes. During games, team staff assistants record television feeds via videocassette, and categorize the results for the players and the team's coaching staff to analyze at a later time.

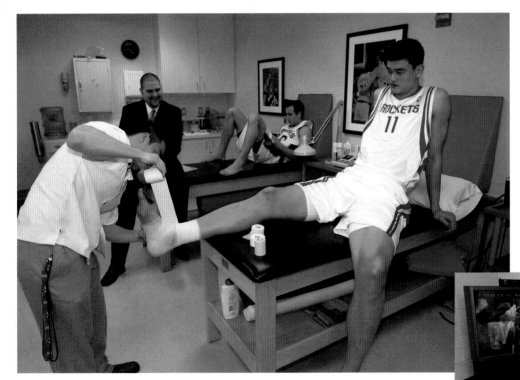

Yao Ming of the Houston Rockets gets his ankle taped in the Staples Center training room prior to the got milk? Rookie Challenge on the 2004 All-Star Weekend in Los Angeles. The training room is an important stop for virtually all NBA players, injured or otherwise.

A few hours before tipoff of a home game, Kobe Bryant scouts the opposing team via a big-screen television located in the Lakers' player lounge at the Staples Center.

The Court

BEFORE THE EXCITEMENT of a basketball game can begin, many arrangements must be made—and not just by coaches and players. The arena must be adequately prepared to host a professional contest, and that can involve a lot of details. First and foremost is the field of play—the game court, which must match uniform league specifications. Next come the preparations needed for all related media, which relays what is happening on the court to the fans, who should be comfortable in their various seats. Finally, in order to keep up with the action during the game, players must have state-of-the-art scoreboards that feature all of the stats most pertinent to the flow of the game, as well as a place to view instant replays.

Magazine, newspaper, and team- and league-employed photographers are present at every game and are usually seated along both of the baselines.

Through video boards like this one at New York's Madison Square Garden, highlights and replays can be shown to an arena crowd instantaneously.

INSIDE THE ARENA

There are several requirements that every NBA arena must have and the court, the baskets, and the scoreboards are all subject to uniform size specifications. All NBA courts are made of durable maple hardwood strips, although there are several possible patterns used by different teams, the most unique being the alternating squares of the parquet design at Boston's FleetCenter.

The only place in a basketball arena that is watched as much as the court itself is the scoreboard, one of the game's most obvious uses of modern technology. Scoreboards have gone from being able to indicate little other than the score and time of game to offering all kinds of information simultaneously: score, time, timeouts remaining, player points, player fouls, shot clocks, time-of-day clocks, as well as team sponsors.

Technology has also allowed for numerous photo-ready angles that rarely could have been captured a decade ago. Before every game, photographers set up remote cameras located above and behind the glass backboards in order to get the most unique shots possible. Then they seat themselves in a row behind the court's baselines.

Arenas also feature their own cameramen, who help create the closed-circuit television feed that is beamed over the video scoreboards for the arena audience. Other video cameramen roam the arena, often beaming their images directly to their production trailer and from there, via satellite, to viewers' homes. Nationally televised games

COURT DIAGRAM

The official NBA diagram shows all of the lines and zones on an NBA court. (WNBA, college, high-school, and international lines are slightly different.) Each area has a role in the game. The free-throw line is the spot where foul shots are set up. The lane between the basket and the free-throw line has a time limit during regular play; offensive players can keep the ball there no longer than three seconds before taking a shot. And three-point shots must be taken from beyond the arc, (22ft/6.7m from the basket in the corners, 23ft 6in/7.2m from the top of the key).

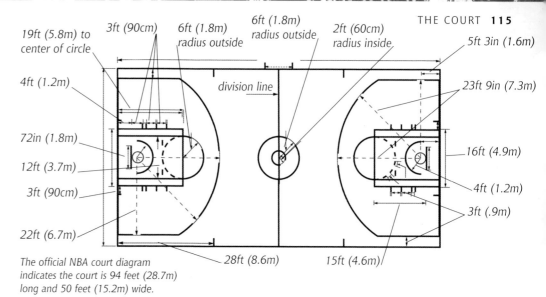

19ft (5.8m) to center of circle
3ft (90cm)
6ft (1.8m) radius outside
6ft (1.8m) radius outside
2ft (60cm) radius inside
5ft 3in (1.6m)
4ft (1.2m)
division line
23ft 9in (7.3m)
72in (1.8m)
16ft (4.9m)
12ft (3.7m)
4ft (1.2m)
3ft (90cm)
3ft (.9m)
22ft (6.7m)
28ft (8.6m)
15ft (4.6m)

The official NBA court diagram indicates the court is 94 feet (28.7m) long and 50 feet (15.2m) wide.

Opening in 1999, Atlanta's Philips Arena is one of the most modern facilities, featuring 96 luxury suites and 20,000 seats, about 12,000 of them in the lower level.

feature a cameraman on the court, often seated at mid-court directly in front of the scorers' table.

Fans can't help but notice the goings-on at the scorers' table. Those usually seated at the table include scorekeepers, league officials, broadcasters, journalists, public-address announcers, and team administrators.

Kendall Gill leans on the scorers table, a popular spot for players waiting for a substitution call.

SEATING

Wooden seats, such as these from the original Madison Square Garden, are now a thing of the past. What started with benches and simple wooden fold-up chairs has evolved over time into a situation that is much more comfortable and practical for fans.

Today's seats are equipped with cushioning, cup-holders, even Internet connections. With the increasing size of the newest scoreboards and videoboards, fans can feel even closer to the action, regardless of their seat location. Some seating areas receive waiter service, but those fans lucky enough to be seated in luxury suites get their own televisions, food catering, and restrooms.

The NBA and the Media

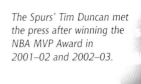

The Spurs' Tim Duncan met the press after winning the NBA MVP Award in 2001–02 and 2002–03.

DURING THE NBA'S EARLY DAYS, fans often found it difficult to follow their favorite team, especially on road trips. Today, however, thanks to technology, basketball is never far from its fans. Every NBA game is broadcast on television and radio, which helps to satisfy the public hunger for all things basketball. Some NBA players transcend the sport, like rapper/actor Shaquille O' Neal. Magazines highlight the personalities that make today's game so dynamic. And thanks to NBA.com, the game is always just a mouse click away, in nine different languages.

"COACH, ONE LAST QUESTION..."

For the media, the buzzer is not the end of the game, but the cue to tell the story of what just occurred. The head coaches almost always figure prominently in that story.

NBA coaches such as Phil Jackson (second from top at right) find themselves surrounded by microphones after every game.

"What strategy did you use? Do you regret starting that player? How did you win the game without your star?"

Deadlines beckon, so questions fly as reporters crowd around the coaches, who are no less popular before games and after practice, although the setting is more relaxed as there is less of a rush.

Some coaches enjoy the give and take; others merely endure the process, recognizing it as a necessary part of their job. Some coaches use the media to convey messages, either to their own players or to opponents. Win or lose, players are often motivated by their coach's critique in the media following a game.

In the end, coaches and the media have a symbiotic relationship: media coverage helps feed basketball's popularity, while coaches' quotes help the media do their job.

AND THE WINNER IS

After the regular season ends, the playoffs start. Around the time of the conference finals, a second, parallel season begins in the NBA—awards season. That is when the league honors the top players from the previous season, along with an award for the NBA Coach of the Year.

Honors also include being part of the All-NBA Teams, All-NBA Defensive Team, and the NBA Rookie of the Year. Print and broadcast media members receive a ballot to write in the players they think are deserving. Those with the most votes are slotted accordingly.

The most coveted award, of course, is the NBA Most Valuable Player trophy, for which a panel of sportswriters in the US and Canada vote. After the votes are tallied, Commissioner David Stern presents the Maurice Podoloff Trophy (named after the NBA's first president) to the winner.

In 2004, Kevin Garnett won the MVP Award by a landslide.

Shaquille O'Neal shares a laugh with Jay Leno during one of his appearances on "The Tonight Show."

STAR POWER

Pro basketball players are great athletes, but they are also entertainers, and therefore often transcend the sport. Wilt Chamberlain once performed on American Bandstand. Michael Jordan achieved worldwide stardom with his play, appearing in a multitude of commercials and even a major motion picture.

The first player to receive true star treatment, however, was George Mikan of the Minneapolis Lakers. The All-Star center was

so popular that when the Lakers visited the New York Knicks, the Madison Square Garden marquee highlighted the matchup, "George Mikan vs. the New York Knicks."

Los Angeles Laker Shaquille O'Neal enjoys star status previously accorded only to movie stars and rock stars. Shaq's exploits on and off the court (he's a rapper and an actor) have given him a larger-than-life persona. Fans can find Shaq on ESPN and on "Entertainment Tonight," on MTV as well as TNT.

A GREAT STORY

Basketball is not just for sports magazines. The newsstand features stories about the NBA and its players in a diverse group of publications. Basketball stars, like all big-name entertainers, are the objects of endless fascination. What does their house look like? What kind of car do they drive?

Moreover, basketball's appeal is not limited to the US. Editors want to sell magazines and what better way than a cover shot of an international superstar whose fan base knows no global borders?

But why does basketball have such broad appeal? Even readers who don't know the difference

between a pick-and-roll and a give-and-go love great stories, and basketball has plenty of those. Michael Jordan getting cut from his high-school team or Yao Ming drawing inspiration from watching Hakeem Olajuwon play on television for the first time are just two. Every player has a great story to tell.

Inside Stuff and Hoop *have pro basketball covered from every angle.*

Left to right: The New York Times Magazine *featured Amaré Stoudemire on its cover, Kevin Garnett called to fans from the cover of the* Japanese Basketball Digest, *and Yao Ming became a* Time *magazine centerpiece.*

NBA MAGAZINES

Can't get enough of pro basketball? The NBA understands. That's why the league produces two magazines: *Hoop*, which features profiles of the hardwood's biggest names accompanied by the best basketball photography anywhere, and *Inside Stuff*, a magazine for young adults. Both magazines go inside the game, giving fans an all-access look at the biggest stars in the NBA.

HOT PROPERTY

On March 2, 1962, the night Wilt Chamberlain scored 100 points, not a single newspaper reporter covered the game. No chance of that happening now. Every NBA game today is covered in detail by newspapers, television stations, and radio broadcasters from around the world, making these media credentials the most sought-after in sports.

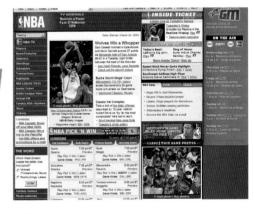

NBA.COM

For hoops fans, there is only one stop on the Internet: NBA.com, where they can find the latest news, live audio and streaming video, player biographies, a history of the sport and past teams and coaches, and much more.

An average of 2 million fans visit the site every day, making NBA.com a premier sports destination on the World Wide Web.

More than half the traffic to the site comes from outside the US, with 26 percent of those visitors coming from Asia alone.

Broadcasting the Game

THE NBA ON ESPN RADIO

BASKETBALL HAS BEEN ON TELEVISION from the beginning of the medium, but never like this. Every NBA game is on the radio and television somewhere; many are telecast around the globe. Game announcers and studio commentators have become as popular as the players themselves. On January 22, 2002, the NBA reached six-year agreements with ABC, ESPN, and Time Warner to have ABC, ESPN, Turner Network Television (TNT), and a new Time Warner/NBA jointly owned, national cable sports network televise NBA games beginning with the 2002–03 season. You can't miss them.

FROM LEFT TO RIGHT ON THE DIAL
The tradition of radio announcers painting pictures with words continues to this day. Fans who can't watch the game can still follow all the action thanks to ESPN Radio, which broadcasts 24 regular-season games and all the playoff action. ESPN Radio has affiliates from coast to coast, ensuring that NBA fans everywhere stay plugged in. ESPN Radio also broadcasts games on the Armed Forces Radio Network to US military personnel worldwide.

NBA ANNOUNCERS
Basketball announcers have always been a part of the show, from Chick Hearn and Johnny Most to today's microphone stars. Most's legendary call from the Celtics' victory in the 1965 NBA Playoffs ("Havlicek stole the ball! Havlicek stole the ball!") still resonates 40 years later. Hearn coined such terms as "slam dunk" and "airball" (to name just a couple)

during his 3,338 consecutive broadcasts of Lakers games. Both men became symbols of their respective franchises.

Today's announcers often pull double duty: Marv Albert announces for TNT and for the Knicks. Many are former players, such as ESPN's Bill Walton. Then there is Al Michaels, already considered one of the best in the business long before he became ABC's lead basketball announcer. One thing they have in common: they love this game, and they make it more fun for the rest of us.

NBA TV host Spero Dedes discusses the art of officiating with Ronnie Nunn, the NBA's Director of Officials.

MUST-SEE TV
In 1999, the NBA launched NBA TV, the all-access channel for everything basketball. Highlights, news, analysis, history, original programming—it all can be found there, along with four NBA games every week.

In 2003–04, NBA TV aired 96 regular-season games, including 40 games that were broadcast live in high-definition format (HDTV), as well as playoff games. NBA TV also airs games from the WNBA, NBDL, and international leagues like FIBA. The network currently reaches 39 countries and 66 million homes worldwide.

Marv Albert's catchphrases have been a part of NBA broadcasts for 25 years.

Bill Walton and Brent Musburger broadcast games for ESPN.

Doc Rivers and Al Michaels formed ABC's lead NBA announcing team in 2003–04.

"LET'S SEND IT BACK TO ERNIE"

NBA games are no longer just 48-minute contests; they are events, with pregame, halftime, and postgame analysis from a regular group of commentators for fans who can't get enough of basketball. The broadcasts have also received critical acclaim: TNT's studio show, "Inside the NBA," won an Emmy.

In 2003–04, TNT's crew of Ernie Johnson, Charles Barkley, and Kenny Smith completed their fourth season. Kevin Frazer and Greg Anthony headline the studio show for ESPN, which completed its second season of broadcasting NBA games in 2003–04. On ABC, John Saunders hosted "NBA Hangtime" in 2003–04 with Tom Tolbert and Byron Scott.

SIDELINE REPORTERS

The newest addition to NBA broadcasts is the sideline reporter, and he or she is truly in the middle of the action (demonstrated above as TNT's Craig Sager interviews Chris Webber from the court). That kind of access allows the reporter to take fans inside the game like never before, even taking viewers into the huddle as the coach draws up the last shot during a time-out.

Offering equal doses of humor and analysis, TNT's studio show—which features (from left to right) Magic Johnson, Ernie Johnson, Kenny Smith, and Charles Barkley—has become a fan favorite.

NATIONWIDE BROADCASTS? TRY WORLDWIDE

Basketball has come a long way and now extends to every corner of the earth. Consider that NBA games air in 212 countries and territories, including Japan, Italy, Russia, Turkey, Iceland, and Germany. The games are broadcast to more than 3.1 billion viewers in 42 languages (see chart at far right).

In 2003–04, NBA games were regularly broadcast to China, Belarus, Georgia, Armenia, Brazil, Poland, and Lithuania for the first time. The broadcasts to China gave that country's 314 million households the first chance to see fellow countryman Yao Ming play for the Houston Rockets in the center position.

In 2004, 325 international media members from 41 different countries and territories covered the NBA All-Star Game in Los Angeles. The game was broadcast live to 212 countries by 103 broadcasters, including

International-language broadcasts of NBA games have become commonplace. In the forefront, an announcing team from CCTV calls a game for viewers in China.

35 that had announcing crews on site ready to interview players and coaches.

The international popularity of basketball is reflected not only in the names on every roster in the NBA, but also with the number of countries broadcasting the league's action, as well as international basketball games.

NBA LANGUAGES

Arabic	Hungarian
Armenian	Icelandic
Bahasa Indonesia	Italian
Bahasa Malaysia	Japanese
Belorussian	Kazakh
Bulgarian	Korean
Cantonese	Lithuanian
Catalan	Macedonian
Creole	Mandarin
Czech	Norwegian
Danish	Polish
Dutch	Portuguese
English	Romanian
Finnish	Russian
Flemish	Serbian
French	Slovak
Georgian	Spanish
German	Swedish
Greek	Tagalog
Hebrew	Thai
Hindi	Turkish

Sponsorship

IMAGINE A BUSINESS with a global brand that is priceless, a brand that appeals to men and women of all ages in virtually every corner of the world. The NBA has such a brand, which is why the league is such an attractive partner for sponsors. Fifteen of the league's 21 marketing partners can be found on the Forbes 500 list and/or the S&P 500. It's an affiliation that pays for both the NBA and its partners, as 62 percent of Americans can identify an NBA sponsor. The league also initiates sponsorship opportunities with Rhythm N' Rims, an interactive tour featuring basketball and music, and an all-around experience of video games and related media called the Jam Van.

The Mavericks' Dirk Nowitzki (above) represents American Express in his homeland of Germany, while Reebok made a shoe for Allen Iverson (right).

The Celtics' forward Paul Pierce helped inflate sales for Spalding's Infusion Basketball.

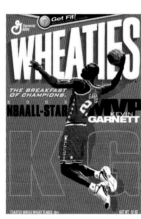

Wheaties tipped off a two-year campaign of NBA-themed packaging with Kevin Garnett.

Got milk? The Nets' Jason Kidd sported a mustache to make the pitch for calcium and healthy bones.

DOMESTIC ADS

A big part of the NBA's fan base is affluent and multicultural—just the audience companies want to reach in order to sell their products. There can be no better way to reach that audience than by pairing with the NBA and one or more of its star players.

Of the NBA's 21 marketing partners, 16 produced new ads for the 2003–04 season. Those ads featured 30 players, just a little less than half of the more than 70 current NBA players participating in marketing campaigns. These players also see big boosts to their income through sponsorship deals.

The appeal of NBA players relative to other professional athletes is illustrated by the fact that 40 of all of sports' 50 best-selling jerseys are those of NBA players. Players' likenesses and team logos have appeared on numerous products utilized or marketed by sponsors such as footwear, cereal boxes, books, video games, print ads, and billboards.

INTERNATIONAL ADS

Basketball is a universal language, which is why sponsors tap NBA stars for overseas marketing campaigns as well. The favorites, of course, are international NBA players promoting products in their home country, such as Dirk Nowitzki in Germany. And there are plenty of international players: NBA rosters featured 73 international players from 34 countries or territories when the 2003–04 season opened.

But the popularity of the game and its players transcends any borders, making Yao Ming a hot commodity in China, the US, and around the world. After his first NBA season of 2002–03, Yao had already been prominently featured in campaigns for Nike, Apple, Gatorade, and Visa.

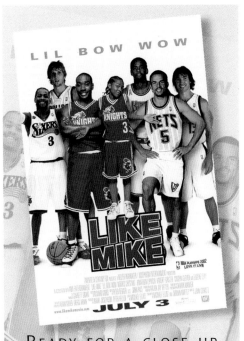

READY FOR A CLOSE-UP

Basketball stars are entertainers, so it's natural that some are in movies. Hank Luisetti played opposite Betty Grable in a 1938 film. Michael Jordan and other NBA stars played opposite Bugs Bunny in 1996's *Space Jam*. *Like Mike* (above) featured rapper Lil Bow Wow as a boy who is transformed into an NBA star after putting on Michael Jordan's shoes.

JAM VAN

The NBA Jam Van is a specially designed, 67-foot-long 18-wheeler that transforms into 8,000 square feet of fun. It tours the US during the spring and summer, stopping in cities to offer young people an interactive NBA experience—for free. The Jam Van's offerings include NBA Jam Van Video Arcade, in which fans can play one-on-one; "NBA's Greatest Plays" Video Screen, which allows fans to

Step right up for the NBA Jam Van, which allows young fans to experience basketball through a variety of free interactive offerings.

choose the plays they want to see using touch-screen technology; "Measure Up" activities in which youngsters can compare their hand and shoe sizes to those of NBA and WNBA players; and NBA Jam Van Partner Area, where fans can receive free samples and product demonstrations.

RHYTHM 'N RIMS

Music and basketball have often been paired, but never like this. NBA Rhythm 'N Rims presented by Sprite is a basketball and music tour that journeys across America in a special 18-wheeler, which transforms into a basketball court and concert stage. The Rhythm 'N Rims truck gives fans the chance to play to their own soundtrack as they compete in a variety of contests: best dribbling moves, slam dunks on 9- and 10-foot rims, free throws, three-pointers, halfcourt shots, and the 24/7 challenge (24 seconds to score 7 points).

Stars from the NBA and WNBA host the events and provide tips for the competitors. All this goes on while some of the biggest names in music perform live. At Rhythm 'N Rims, fans can become part of the action.

At the NBA Rhythms 'N Rims, fans can compete in a variety of skills contests, including a slam-dunk competition.

Collectibles

IN ADDITION TO THE KNOWLEDGE gained from having seen an NBA game in person, chances are that those leaving the arena will not be doing so empty-handed. Between team-related merchandise, game programs, and ticket stubs, there are plenty of ways to literally take the game home with you. Collecting sports memorabilia and gear has become an industry and world unto itself, and there are plenty of NBA-licensed goods out in the market. Whether it's about team loyalty, the sentimental value of a memento, practicality, or simply a collector's investment, everyone loves to show their team colors.

TICKET STUBS

While some fans have always collected ticket stubs from NBA events they have attended, it is only recently that stubs have started being produced with their collectible worth in mind.

Some ticket stubs alternate between photos of players (as on the ticket for a home Philadelphia 76ers game, above left) and team legends and fans (above right), while others contain team logos.

As to the rest of a ticket stub, only a few things have changed over time, most obviously the unique barcodes that have been added so they can be scanned for authenticity.

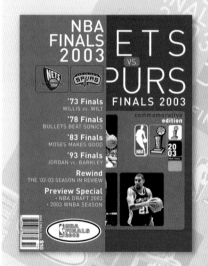

EVENT PROGRAMS

Commemorative programs are some of the most desired collectibles of any of the NBA's big events. In addition to extensive coverage on both conference champions and past Finals records and stats, the annual Finals programs feature a letter from Commissioner David Stern, a month-by-month season review, a draft preview, season award-winners, anniversary stories, as well as a WNBA season preview and the Read to Achieve initiative. The All-Star Program features local flavor, highlighting the host city and franchise, whether it's great players, moments, or teams.

GAME PROGRAMS

When it comes to getting information about what's going on at an NBA game, few things can be as helpful as a good game program. Lineups, feature stories, and team information are at the heart of these publications, but they also are collectibles in their own right.

With local content, such as team-specific stories and advertisements, game programs these days also feature a national edition of *Hoop* magazine, an official periodical of the NBA. They can be purchased on the concourse at games and are occasionally given free of charge to season-ticket holders.

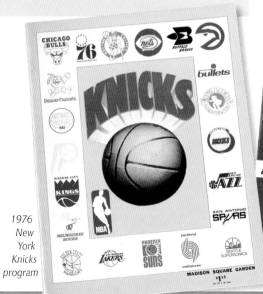

1976 New York Knicks program

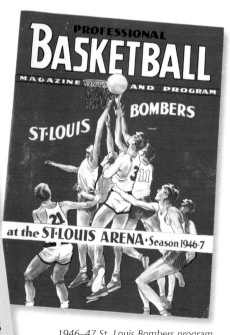

1946–47 St. Louis Bombers program

TEAM CONCESSIONS

All NBA arenas include specific places where fans can buy home-team merchandise, whether it's from licensed vendors or the official team store. They can find everything from authentic and replica uniforms to bobblehead dolls and everyday accessories like pencils and pens, all of which sport the logo of their favorite team or a likeness of their favorite player. Other examples include: shooting shirts, socks, sweatshirts, throwback uniforms, sports bags, headbands, wristbands, bench towels, personalized gear, event-specific gear (for playoffs, All-Star Games, or Finals), watches, team yearbooks, media guides, adult and children's books, and even décor like wallpaper and flags. Often, there is selected merchandise for the visiting team as well.

With the widespread distribution of team gear to retailers and the recent arrival of the NBA Store, it is possible to find unique examples of team merchandise nearly anywhere at any time. (The NBA Store is located at the intersection of 5th Avenue and 52nd Street in New York and at nba.com.)

The official Team L.A. Store at Staples Center features nearly every type of Lakers' merchandise and memorabilia in existence.

Basketball bowl and glass

Foam finger

Allen Iverson celebriduck

Nets mascot (Sly Fox) bobblehead doll

Shaquille O'Neal bobblehead doll

Fans have a plethora of team headgear to chose from at one of the Team L.A. Stores in the Los Angeles area.

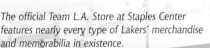

Game-Night Extras

AT AN NBA GAME, the on-court action that has fans riveted to their seats doesn't start and end with the actual game. There's an inherent glamour to the entertainment that is modern professional basketball, and this has never been clearer than in recent years, when top-level acts have performed national anthems and halftime shows. Meanwhile, fans can be entertained by team mascots, dance teams and cheerleaders, as well as the on-court contests taking place during media timeouts.

GAME-NIGHT PERFORMANCES

The honor of being chosen to sing the "The Star-Spangled Banner" during NBA Playoffs and All-Star Games, makes it a desirable venue for even the world's biggest stars. Many rising stars, often local talent, are also given the opportunity to perform the vocally demanding tune throughout the season at the league's various arenas. Modern technology and lots of good old-fashioned planning have made it possible for nearly full-scale concerts to take place in NBA arenas during half times. Although getting the equipment on and off of the court in a reasonable amount of time can be a difficult logistical issue, Jewel, Joan Jett and the Blackhearts, and Sheryl Crow are among those who have performed to game-night audiences.

Multi-platinum singer and songwriter Brian McKnight sings the National Anthem prior to the season home opener between the Minnesota Timberwolves and the Milwaukee Bucks.

Jewel performs during half time of Game 3 of the 2003 NBA Finals between the San Antonio Spurs and the New Jersey Nets.

MASCOTS

Regardless of how their favorite team fared, fans of all ages can be sure that they will be entertained by the exploits of the various team mascots who make the NBA game-night experience as fun as it can be.

Whether the Phoenix Suns' Gorilla (above) throws down one acrobatic dunk after another, the Philadelphia 76ers' Hip-Hop shoots t-shirts into the stands, or the Boston Celtics' Lucky the Leprechaun takes a breather in a celebrity's courtside seat, team mascots always provide a very memorable night.

Actor and rapper Will Smith, a Philadelphia native, helps team mascot Hip-Hop slingshoot shirts into the crowd at a home 76ers game.

DANCERS

A trip to an NBA game is a rhythm- and music-filled experience, and nothing personifies that more than the professional dance teams performing at every NBA home game. Nearly all team dancers boast professional performing credits including videos, tours, television, film, and theater. Many are even classically trained.

Working with top directors and choreographers, NBA dance teams give fans another reason to cheer, whether it's before, during, or after games, or at team-related and community functions.

The Dallas Mavericks' Mavs Dancers are one of many team-affiliated dance teams entertaining fans in NBA arenas. Most NBA teams also feature cheerleading squads and mascots.

ON-COURT CONTESTS

Whether it's a race, team trivia, a "basketball tug of war" in which two fans must shoot baskets while connected by a bungee cord, or a "shoot for a free flight to the city of your choice" contest, the various competitions and games held for prizes on the court during media timeouts and quarter breaks can be as entertaining as they are rewarding. Performed by fans randomly chosen by their section and seat numbers, these contests are supervised by promotional staff members of NBA teams and have been a staple at games for years.

A race of fans inside giant inflatable hamster-balls is just one of the various on-court contests that can be seen at NBA games.

All for the Fans

THE PLAYERS KNOW IT, the coaches know it, and the league knows it: the NBA experience would be nowhere near what it is without its fans. There are plenty of benefits to life as a fan besides watching the on-court action. Teams, with the help of sponsors, often feature giveaway promotions. Also, die-hard fans dress the part and often employ creative signs in an attempt to visibly support their team—and hopefully get on TV. Many other courtside regulars are at the top of their professions, whether it's stage, screen, business, media, fashion, or even other sports, and many cheer just as loudly as the fans with painted faces. Most recently, with global games, international fans have joined the mix as well.

A young fan holds a bobblehead doll of Phoenix Sun Shawn Marion during a 2002 game in Phoenix, Arizona.

FANS DRESS UP

There are plenty of ways to support one's team, but none is more obvious (or more of a magnet for TV cameras) than dressing the part. Whether it's face and body painting, or just wearing the uniform (there are plenty of types of game-authentic, replica, and retro-reissue "throwback" apparel available for every NBA team), you're certain to see plenty of it on any given night in an NBA arena.

Sometimes, those who have been die-hard fans the longest can be spotted by identifying their original "retro" gear.

A painted group of Dallas Mavericks fans rally outside of a 2003 Western Conference Semifinals game at American Airlines Center in Dallas, Texas.

GIVEAWAYS

One of the great perks of attending NBA games is receiving giveaway items, usually provided by the team and a sponsor and given away nightly or on special promotion nights. Among the most popular promotions are bobblehead dolls (modeled after players, coaches, or mascots), inflatable noisemaker sticks, mini-balls, towels, shirts, and hats. Team posters, trading cards, and magnetic schedules are also sometimes among the freebies.

Mavs fans make some noise with their "thunder sticks" as the Dallas Mavericks host the Portland Trail Blazers in Game One of the Western Conference Quarterfinals during the 2003 NBA Playoffs.

Spike Lee (left) and Chris Rock attend one of Lee's beloved New York Knicks games. He's a staple at their home games in Madison Square Garden.

INTERNATIONAL FANS

Basketball is truly a global sport, as is evidenced by the diverse crowd in an NBA arena on any given night. Similar to Broadway shows, NBA games are popular sightseeing stops for many international citizens visiting North America. International stars in the league also attract tourists, as seen by the number of Chinese flags waved whenever Yao Ming hits a shot at Houston Rockets games.

This Japanese fan smiles as he shows off a commemorative shirt autographed by players during the 2003 NBA Japan Games in Tokyo.

CELEBRITY FANS

Some years back, a clip of Jack Nicholson cheering on a young Magic Johnson made the game-highlight package that was broadcast on television, and the way celebrities are seen in public was forever changed. A who's-who of filmmakers (Spike Lee, Steven Spielberg, and Penny Marshall), actors and actresses (Denzel Washington, Dyan Cannon, and James Gandolfini), musicians (Beyoncé Knowles, Jay-Z, and Jimmy Buffett), business magnates (Calvin Klein, Bill Gates, and Russell Simmons), and professional athletes (Derek Jeter, Michael Strahan, and Lance Armstrong) are among those to attend many games per season, nearly all of them in the best seats imaginable.

Jack Nicholson, one of the most decorated and admired actors in the history of the silver screen, has had Laker season tickets longer than any coach or player has been with the team,

NBA Stars Reach out

NOTHING IS MORE IMPORTANT in professional sports than the fans. The NBA, WNBA, and NBDL teams, coaches, and players know that a large part of their duties as professionals include promoting the game of basketball, connecting with fans, and making a difference in their respective communities. While signing autographs remains a popular way of interacting with fans, foundations and charities organized by teams and individuals, as well as such initiatives as the Read to Achieve program (which reaches approximately 50 million children a year), Jr. NBA/Jr. WNBA, and Destination Finals, are helping fans and communities in more ways than ever before.

The foundation set up by Laker Gary Payton provides Thanksgiving dinners to disadvantaged citizens of L.A..

GOODWILL FOUNDATIONS

While all players make a difference on the court, some also make a difference off of it. Many have their own foundations that spread goodwill year-round in their communities. Through foundations set up by the NBA, WNBA, and NBDL, teams, coaches, and players invest time and money in initiatives that deal with issues such as literacy and education, hunger, poverty, housing, and cancer. Some players reach out past their franchise's cities: Dikembe Mutombo built a hospital in his homeland of the African nation of Congo.

One of the NBA's most popular players, Kevin Garnett takes the time to sign autographs for fans.

AUTOGRAPHS

For fans of all ages, there is no better way to prove they have met their basketball heroes than getting a signature. For those lucky enough to catch a player at the right moment—most often immediately before and after pregame shoot-arounds—they may be able to go home that night with an autograph. From programs, basketball cards, ticket stubs, and posters to shirts and casts, fans ask their heroes to sign a surprising variety of items.

The best steps to securing an autograph are to always be patient and respectful, always have a marker ready, and always have something for the player to write on.

One of the rarest souvenirs anyone can take home from a sporting event is the actual shoe worn by a player, as shown by this youngster who received one from Shaquille O'Neal.

Jr. NBA and Jr. WNBA

The Jr. NBA and Jr. WNBA comprise the league's youth basketball development program, which reaches more than a million kids (ages 5–14) and supports 1,000 recreational basketball leagues in North America and abroad. The program reaches youths through instructional and recognition programs, clinics, player and coach appearances, tournaments, and a new online initiative entitled "Keys to Success."

The Jr. NBA and Jr. WNBA are overseen by an Advisory Council, whose members include NBA players Ray Allen and Mike Bibby, WNBA players Sue Bird and Tina Thompson, officials Danny Crawford and Lisa Mattingly, and NBA legend Bill Walton.

NBA stars Allan Houston, Brendan Haywood, and Lonnie Baxter stand before the White House with members of the Boys and Girls Club of Greater Washington during a Jr. NBA/Jr. WNBA program.

Some of the NBA's all-time greats gathered for an NBA Playoffs viewing party at Center Court of the Naismith Memorial Basketball Hall of Fame in May 2004.

Destination Finals

As part of the 2004 NBA Legends Tour: Destination Finals, NBA legends Bill Russell, Julius Erving, Bill Walton, Clyde Drexler, Moses Malone, George Gervin, Robert Parish, Artis Gilmore, and Spud Webb—who have won a total of 20 NBA and three ABA championships—showcased the Larry O'Brien Trophy. They visited NBA Playoff cities and some non-NBA cities for fan autograph and photo sessions, community projects and events, a series of NBA Playoff viewing parties, and, of course, more than 30 Playoff games.

BASKETBALL TODAY

Basketball today is a global game. By the close of the 2003–04 season, NBA team rosters featured nearly 70 international players from 33 countries and territories, with those numbers undoubtedly set to rise in the future. The world's greatest athletes continue to amaze on the international scene, as well as at home throughout the season and during All-Star Weekend. Shaq, Duncan, Garnett, Kobe, Iverson, McGrady, Nowitzki—along with an influx of new talent such as Yao, LeBron and Carmelo Anthony (both pictured here), and Dwyane Wade—show that the NBA is in good hands for years to come. And with the WNBA approaching it's ten-year anniversary, women's basketball is becoming more popular every year.

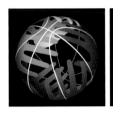

For more than 70 years, FIBA has been the governing body for international competition in basketball.

FIBA

IT DID NOT TAKE LONG for basketball to become a global game. In 1919, players flocked to Paris for the first international tournament. Over the years, the expansion continued unabated, but organization was needed, especially after basketball's acceptance as an Olympic sport in 1930. That led to the 1932 formation of the International Basketball Federation (FIBA), the world's first governing body for basketball. FIBA, which later changed its name to Federation Internationale de Basketball Amateur (FIBA has since dropped Amateur from its name), has grown from eight members in 1932, to 212. Based in Switzerland, the organization stages the world championships for men and women every four years, and oversees Olympic basketball from qualifying events to the gold-medal game.

A smiling Shaquille O'Neal graced the cover of the FIBA guide from the 1996 Olympics in Atlanta, Georgia.

McDonald's Championship

It wasn't until 1987 that an NBA team competed against international teams in a FIBA-sanctioned event. The McDonald's Championship, inaugurated that year in Milwaukee, Wisconsin, featured the Bucks playing the Soviet National Team and Tracer Milan, a prominent Italian team.

Madrid, Rome, Barcelona, and Paris were the next stops for the event, which is held every other year to avoid conflicts with the Olympics and the FIBA World Championships. The structure also has changed: more teams have been added, and the defending NBA champion faces off against five other league champions from around the world.

The New Jersey Nets selected Oscar Schmidt (right) with a sixth round pick in 1984, but he opted to remain in his homeland.

Oscar Schmidt

One of the first international players to earn a worldwide reputation was Brazil's Oscar Schmidt. The 6-8 shooting guard was thought by some to be the greatest player in the world during his 26-year career from 1977–2003. By an unofficial count, Schmidt scored 49,703 points with various clubs and with Brazil's national team—over 11,000 more than NBA scoring leader Kareem Abdul-Jabbar.

Schmidt's crowning achievement was a 46-point outburst during the gold-medal game of the 1987 Pan American Games that led to an upset of the US team in Indianapolis, Indiana.

The Denver Nuggets went head-to-head against top international teams in the 1989 McDonald's Championship, played in Rome. Here the Denver Nuggets defeated Jugoplastika Spalato of Yugoslavia 135-129.

WORLD CHAMPIONSHIP

Basketball fans don't have to wait four years for the best international competition, thanks to the World Basketball Championship, organized by FIBA in 1950, to be held every four years between Olympic games. Argentina hosted the first World Championship and went 5-0 to win that event.

Though the US won the 1954 World Championship, the Americans have not dominated this event like they have in Olympic basketball. Indeed, Brazil followed the US triumph by winning back-to-back World Championships.

In 2002, the US hosted the World Championship for the first time, and 17,000 fans packed Indianapolis' Conseco Fieldhouse to watch Yugoslavia defeat Argentina in overtime. It was their second straight World Championship win.

Vlade Divac and Peja Stojakovic celebrate after leading Yugoslavia to its second straight World Basketball Championship in 2002.

2002 WORLD BASKETBALL CHAMPIONSHIP

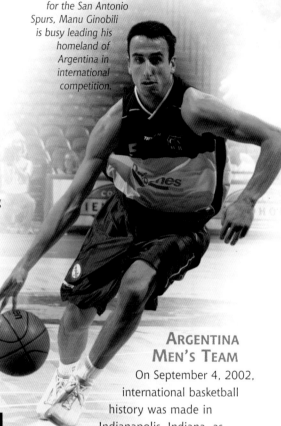

When he's not at point guard for the San Antonio Spurs, Manu Ginobili is busy leading his homeland of Argentina in international competition.

ARGENTINA MEN'S TEAM

On September 4, 2002, international basketball history was made in Indianapolis, Indiana, as Argentina became the first national team to defeat a US team since FIBA allowed NBA players to participate in international competition. They won with an 87-80 victory in an early-round game of the World Championship of Basketball.

The Argentines ultimately took home silver medals, after an 84-77 overtime defeat at the hands of Yugoslavia, but players like guard Emanuel "Manu" Ginobili and forward Andrés Nocioni saw their personal stock rise after going head-to-head against top-level NBA talent and coming out victorious.

It's no wonder that the NBA has begun drafting Argentinean players such as Ginobili and Carlos Delfino into its ranks. With a title in the 2000 World Championship for Young Men, second-place finishes in the 2001 Goodwill Games and 2002 World Championship, third place in the 2001 World Championship for Young Men, and other great performances in recent years, Argentina is becoming one of the most respected international basketball powers.

WOMEN'S WORLD CHAMPIONSHIP

FIBA staged the first women's World Championship in 1953, just three years after the men's event began. An intense US–Soviet rivalry highlighted the first 10 women's World Championships, as each country won the gold medal five times. Brazil ended the rivals' stranglehold on the gold medal by winning the World Championship in 1994, but it

The Chinese women's team displays their silver medals from the 1994 World Championship, the first medals won by their country in a FIBA event.

proved to be only a blip on the radar. The Americans won in 1998 (in Australia) and 2002 (in China), though 2002's gold-medal game proved to be quite a battle, teaching the US women something the men have known for some time: the world is gaining on them.

The Olympics

BASKETBALL MADE ITS OLYMPIC DEBUT at the 1936 Summer Games in Berlin, which was ironic because Dr. James Naismith invented the sport for indoor play during winter. Furthermore, this indoor sport played its first gold-medal game outdoors in the rain. The circumstances may have been a surprise, but the outcome was not: the US defeated Canada 19-8, with the 75-year-old Naismith in attendance. It was the first of seven consecutive gold medals for the Americans. By the 1970s, however, the gap between the US and the rest of the world had narrowed, at least at the amateur level. But not for long. In 1989, FIBA lifted its ban on professional players and Olympic basketball has never been the same.

The 1956 US Olympic team featured Bill Russell (standing, 6th from left) and K. C. Jones (kneeling, 2nd from right), each of whom would go on to Hall of Fame careers with the Boston Celtics.

1956: A TEAM FOR THE AGES

Melbourne, Australia, hosted the 1956 Olympics, and since the seasons are reversed in the Southern Hemisphere, the Summer Games were held in November. But the time of year made no difference to the Americans, who assembled one of the greatest teams in Olympic history.

The US team, a group of amateur collegians led by Bill Russell and his University of San Francisco teammate K. C. Jones, won all eight of its games by an average margin of 55.3 points per game. The Americans capped their run by defeating the Soviets 89-55 in the gold-medal game. Russell returned home in time to play two-thirds of the season for Boston, leading the Celtics to the first of 11 titles as a rookie.

Alexander Belov's layup (far left) gave the Soviets a controversial victory in the 1972 Olympic basketball final, a gold medal that is commemorated by the banner at left.

1972: A CONTROVERSY FOR THE AGES

The game has long since ended, but the debate over the 1972 Olympic basketball final may never die down. The former Soviet Union defeated the US 51-50 in Munich, Germany, but only after officials twice ordered the final three seconds replayed because of confusion over timing and timeouts.

Coached by Oklahoma State's Henry Iba, and featuring such collegiate standouts as Doug Collins and Dwight Jones, the Americans, who thought they had the game won—not only once but twice—could not stop the Soviets on the third try. Alexander Belov won the battle for a length-of-the-court pass and made the winning basket at the buzzer to end the US's 63-game Olympic winning streak.

1992: THE DREAM TEAM

No one doubted that the best basketball in the world could be found nightly in NBA arenas. Where those players couldn't be found, however, was on the Olympic hardwood—at least not until 1992. With the ban on US professionals lifted, USA Basketball put together the "super" all-star team that everyone wanted: in other words, the "Dream Team."

In Barcelona, Spain, site of the 1996 Summer Olympics, the Dream Team transcended sports, receiving a frenzied welcome usually reserved for rock stars while dominating media coverage throughout the two weeks. On the court, opposing players seemed to debate whether they should try to cover the Americans or ask for their autograph (many did both).

The Dream Team proved every bit as good as advertised, rolling to an 8-0 record and winning by an average margin of 43.8 points per game.

The original Dream Team: (back row, left to right) Patrick Ewing, Christian Laettner, Magic Johnson, David Robinson, and Karl Malone; (middle row) Larry Bird, Michael Jordan, Coach Chuck Daly, Charles Barkley, and Chris Mullin; (front row) Scottie Pippen, John Stockton, and Clyde Drexler.

Magic Johnson savors the moment after helping the Dream Team win the gold medal at the 1992 Olympics.

1996: GOLDEN RESULTS

At the 1996 Olympics in Atlanta, Charles Barkley, Karl Malone, David Robinson, Scottie Pippen, and John Stockton returned to headline the second coming of the US Olympic team. Penny Hardaway, Grant Hill, Reggie Miller, Hakeem Olajuwon, Shaquille O'Neal, Gary Payton, and Mitch Richmond joined the them to create another super all-star team. The squad, coached by Lenny Wilkens, lived up to expectations, posting an 8-0 record and winning the gold medal, while defeating opponents by 31.8 points per game.

The US beat Yugoslavia 95-69 in the gold-medal game in front of 34,600 fans at the Georgia Dome to cap off another fantastic run.

In 1996, Charles Barkley helped the US defeat China 133-70 to set an Olympic record for most points in a game.

OLYMPIC MEDALS

MEN

1936
Gold United States
Silver Canada
Bronze Mexico

1948
Gold United States
Silver France
Bronze Brazil

1952
Gold United States
Silver Soviet Union
Bronze Uruguay

1956
Gold United States
Silver Soviet Union
Bronze Uruguay

1960
Gold United States
Silver Soviet Union
Bronze Brazil

1964
Gold United States
Silver Soviet Union
Bronze Brazil

1968
Gold United States
Silver Yugoslavia
Bronze Soviet Union

1972
Gold Soviet Union
Silver United States
Bronze Cuba

1976
Gold United States
Silver Yugoslavia
Bronze Soviet Union

1980
Gold Yugoslavia
Silver Italy
Bronze Soviet Union

1984
Gold United States
Silver Spain
Bronze Yugoslavia

1988
Gold Soviet Union
Silver Yugoslavia
Bronze United States

1992
Gold United States
Silver Croatia
Bronze Lithuania

1996
Gold United States
Silver Yugoslavia
Bronze Lithuania

2000
Gold United States
Silver France
Bronze Lithuania

WOMEN

1976
Gold Soviet Union
Silver United States
Bronze Bulgaria

1980
Gold Soviet Union
Silver Bulgaria
Bronze Yugoslavia

1984
Gold United States
Silver South Korea
Bronze China

1988
Gold United States
Silver Yugoslavia
Bronze Soviet Union

1992
Gold Unified Team*
Silver China
Bronze United States

1996
Gold United States
Silver Brazil
Bronze Australia

2000
Gold United States
Silver Australia
Bronze Brazil

* Former Soviet Union

International Players in the NBA

EVEN FROM DAY ONE, the NBA, then known as the Basketball Association of America, had an international flavor. Hank Biasetti, an Italian-Canadian, played for the Toronto Huskies when they battled the New York Knickerbockers in the league's very first game on November 1, 1946. Yet what started out as an Eastern League in the late 1940s, has flourished into an international sensation, featuring more than 70 players from more than 30 countries from all over the world. Argentina, Congo, France, Lithuania, Senegal, Spain, and Ukraine are just some of the countries that have produced top basketball talent. Whether they come straight into the league or arrive via the college route, the influx of international players has grown considerably since the mid-1980s, and has really blossomed since the late 1990s. With the surge of players continuing, the NBA's global popularity will reach even greater heights.

When he's not scoring for the Denver Nuggets, Nené represents his country (Brazil) in international competition.

COUNTRY	PLAYER	NBA TEAM
Argentina	Carlos Delfino*	Detroit Pistons
	Emanuel "Manu" Ginobili	San Antonio Spurs
	Federico Kammerichs*	Portland Trail Blazers
	Marcelo Nicola*	Portland Trail Blazers
	Luis Scola*	San Antonio Spurs
Australia	David Andersen*	Atlanta Hawks
	Ben Pepper*	Boston Celtics
Belize	Milt Palacio	Toronto Raptors
Bosnia-Herzegovina	Nedzad Sinanovic*	Portland Trail Blazers
Brazil	Nené	Denver Nuggets
	Leandro Barbosa	Phoenix Suns
	Alex Garcia	San Antonio Spurs
Cameroon	Ruben Boumtje Boumtje	Cleveland Cavaliers
Canada	Rick Fox	Los Angeles Lakers
	Todd MacCulloch	Philadelphia 76ers
	Jamaal Magloire	New Orleans Hornets
	Steve Nash	Dallas Mavericks

COUNTRY	PLAYER	NBA TEAM
China	Yao Ming	Houston Rockets
	Xue Yuyang*	Denver Nuggets
	Wang Zhizhi	Miami Heat
Congo	Dikembe Mutombo	New York Knicks
Croatia	Gordan Giricek	Utah Jazz
	Mario Kasun*	Orlando Magic
	Toni Kukoc	Milwaukee Bucks
	Zoran Planinic	New Jersey Nets
	Josip Sesar*	Boston Celtics
Czech Republic	Jiri Welsch	Boston Celtics
England	Andrew Betts*	New Orleans Hornets
	Ndudi Ebi	Minnesota Timberwolves
France	Tariq Abdul-Wahad	Dallas Mavericks
	Boris Diaw-Riffiod	Atlanta Hawks
	Alain Digbeu*	Atlanta Hawks
	Jerome Moiso	Toronto Raptors
	Paccelis Morlende*	Seattle SuperSonics
	Tony Parker	San Antonio Spurs
	Mickael Pietrus	Golden State Warriors
	Frederic Weis*	New York Knicks

COUNTRY	PLAYER	NBA TEAM
Georgia	Zaza Pachulia	Orlando Magic
	Vladimir Stepania	Portland Trail Blazers
	Nikoloz Tskitishvili	Denver Nuggets
Germany	Peter Fehse*	Seattle SuperSonics
	Dirk Nowitzki	Dallas Mavericks
Greece	Andreas Glyniadakis*	Detroit Pistons
	Sofoklis Schortsanitis*	Los Angeles Clippers
	Iakovos "Jake" Tsakalidis	Memphis Grizzlies
Haiti	Samuel Dalembert	Philadelphia 76ers
Iceland	Jon Stefansson	Dallas Mavericks
Lithuania	Zydrunas Ilgauskas	Cleveland Cavaliers
	Robertas Javtokas*	San Antonio Spurs
	Darius Songaila	Sacramento Kings
	Aurelijius Zukauskas*	Milwaukee Bucks
Mexico	Eduardo Najera	Dallas Mavericks
Netherlands	Francisco Elson	Denver Nuggets
	Dan Gadzuric	Milwaukee Bucks
	Remon Van de Hare*	Orlando Magic
New Zealand	Sean Marks	San Antonio Spurs
Nigeria	Obinna Ekezie	Atlanta Hawks
	Michael Olowokandi	Minnesota Timberwolves
Poland	Maciej Lampe	Phoenix Suns
	Szymon Szewczyk*	Milwaukee Bucks
	Cezary Trybanski	New York Knicks
Puerto Rico	Carlos Arroyo	Utah Jazz
	Daniel Santiago	Milwaukee Bucks
Russia	Andrei Fetisov*	Milwaukee Bucks
	Andrei Kirilenko	Utah Jazz
Scotland	Robert Archibald	Toronto Raptors
Senegal	Malick Badiane*	Houston Rockets
	DeSagana Diop	Cleveland Cavaliers
	Mamadou N'diaye	Atlanta Hawks
Serbia and Montenegro	Dejan Bodiroga*	Sacramento Kings
	Zarko Cabarkapa	Phoenix Suns
	Vlade Divac	Sacramento Kings
	Predrag Drobnjak	Los Angeles Clippers
	Marko Jaric	Los Angeles Clippers
	Nenad Krstic*	New Jersey Nets
	Darko Milicic	Detroit Pistons
	Aleksandar Pavlovic	Utah Jazz
	Vladimir Radmanovic	Seattle SuperSonics
	Zeljko Rebraca	Atlanta Hawks
	Mladen Sekularac	Dallas Mavericks
	Predrag "Peja" Stojakovic	Sacramento Kings
	Milos Vujanic*	Phoenix Suns

COUNTRY	PLAYER	NBA TEAM
Slovenia	Primoz Brezec	Indiana Pacers
	Bostjan Nachbar	Houston Rockets
	Radoslav "Rasho" Nesterovic	San Antonio Spurs
	Sani Becirovic*	Denver Nuggets
Spain	Roberto Duenas*	New Orleans Hornets
	Pau Gasol	Memphis Grizzlies
	Raul Lopez	Utah Jazz
	Juan Carlos Navarro*	Washington Wizards
St. Vincent and the Grenadines	Adonal Foyle	Golden State Warriors
Turkey	Mehmet Okur	Detroit Pistons
	Hidayet "Hedo" Turkoglu	San Antonio Spurs
Ukraine	Stanislav Medvedenko	Los Angeles Lakers
	Vitaly Potapenko	Seattle SuperSonics
US Virgin Islands	Raja Bell	Utah Jazz
	Tim Duncan	San Antonio Spurs

*Players from around the world whose rights are held by an NBA team

One of the heroes of the 2003 NBA Finals, Manu Ginobili of the San Antonio Spurs earned a reputation as a premier international player as a member of Argentina's National Team.

All-Star MVPs

THE ALL-STAR GAME BEGAN as a potential money-losing proposition in the early 1950s, and developed into one of sports' biggest global events by the turn of the century. In the 50-plus years of All-Star Games, many moments have stood out, including Easy Ed Macauley taking home the first All-Star Game MVP honors in 1951, Wilt Chamberlain's inaugural MVP All-Star performance in 1960, and Magic's 1992 inspirational MVP performance only three months after announcing his retirement from the game. Year after year, All-Star greatness brings unforgettable moments.

MR. ALL-STAR MVP

The greatest power forward of his era was also a premier All-Star performer. Bob Pettit of the St. Louis Hawks used the All-Star Game as his personal showcase to display his vast all-around skills. The 1955 NBA Rookie of the Year won an unsurpassed four MVP awards and set several records, including those for most rebounds in a quarter (10), half (16), and game (27). The Baton Rouge, Louisiana, native averaged 20.4 points in 11 games throughout his Hall of Fame career.

THE FIRST ALL-STAR GAME

Few believed an All-Star Game would be a success except Walter Brown. In 1952, the Boston Celtics' visionary owner was steadfast in his belief that an All-Star Game was a good idea, even though professional basketball was struggling to attract fans.

So Brown covered the expenses and hosted the first-ever game at Boston Garden. Doubts quickly subsided as 10,094 fans turned out to see Easy Ed Macauley score 20 points and lead the East to a 111-94 victory.

The All-Star Game is now watched by a worldwide audience in over 210 countries.

WILT'S ALL-STAR DEBUT

Wilt Chamberlain burst onto the NBA scene as a rookie with the Philadelphia Warriors in the 1959–60 season, leading the league in scoring (37.6) and rebounding (27.0).

So what did he do at his first NBA All-Star Game in his hometown of Philadelphia? The 7-1 center scored 23 points and pulled down 25 rebounds, earning NBA MVP honors and leading the East to a 125-115 victory.

Chamberlain went on to play in 12 more All-Star Games, yet his smashing debut in 1960 was the only one that netted him MVP honors.

Easy Ed Macauley, Walter Brown, and Bob Cousy all played valuable roles in the NBA's first All-Star Game, which was held in Boston in 1951.

It didn't take Wilt Chamberlain long to establish himself among the NBA's elite players as he thrilled his hometown fans in Philadelphia, earning MVP honors in his first All-Star Game appearance.

In one of the most memorable performances in All-Star Game history, Magic stole the show in his inspirational return to the NBA as he led the West to a 153-113 victory in 1992.

A who's who of All-Star greatness gathered in Washington, DC, during the 2001 All-Star Weekend.

AN MVP COLLECTION

Nearly 4,000 players have logged at least one minute in the NBA over the league's 58-year history, yet the majority have never had the privilege of playing in the ultimate individual showcase—the NBA All-Star Game. Even fewer, of course, have earned the honor of being called the game's greatest player for an afternoon—in each season, there can only be one All-Star MVP. So, in 2001, one of the greatest collections of basketball talent ever assembled gathered in Washington, DC, to celebrate the league's 50th anniversary of the mid-season classic. Twenty-six MVPs had a chance to reminisce about their unique roles in basketball history.

HOMETOWN MVPs

Easy Ed Macauley started the tradition and Shaquille O'Neal kept it alive 53 years later: hometown MVPs. Eleven players have won All-Star Game MVPs in the same city they call their professional home. Bob Pettit, Wilt Chamberlain, Rick Barry, Jerry West, Tom Chambers, Michael Jordan, John Stockton, and Karl Malone are some of the players who have shined the brightest among their All-Star peers while making their hometown crowds proud.

MAGIC'S MAGICAL PERFORMANCE

The emotions were running high on February 9, 1992, as one of the game's greatest players returned to the court a mere three months after announcing he had contracted the human immunodeficiency virus (HIV) that causes AIDS. Magic Johnson mesmerized the sold-out crowd in Orlando, Florida, with a triumphant return, dazzling fans and fellow players with a 25-point performance to earn MVP honors.

Shaquille O'Neal is all smiles after earning All-Star MVP honors in 2004.

All-Star Contests

WHAT STARTED AS A SINGLE EVENT has evolved into a weeklong celebration of All-Star activities and community-service initiatives. The pivotal year in this transformation was 1984, when the Slam Dunk Contest was added a day prior to the NBA All-Star Game. The popularity of the contest spawned other skills competitions, such as the three-point shootout (1986), Rookie Challenge (1994), All-Star Hoop It Up (2002), and the Skills Challenge (2003), all of which have become a part of NBA All-Star lore.

Even though he won the NBA's Rookie of the Year honor in 1999, Vince Carter ascended to a new level of celebrity when he won the 2000 Slam Dunk Contest.

One of basketball's preeminent dunkers, Michael Jordan mesmerized fans and foes alike with his gravity-defying moves—such as this one from the 1987 Slam Dunk Contest held in Seattle, Washington.

THE ELEVATORS

The art of elevation was raised to a new level in 1984 when the NBA introduced the Slam Dunk Contest in Denver, which also happened to be the site of the first dunk contest launched nine years earlier by the rival American Basketball Association. In that '75 contest, Julius Erving set a new standard against which all dunkers were measured when he ran and took off from the free-throw line to throw it down the basket, much to the delirious delight of the Denver fans in attendance.

Thirteen years later, Michael Jordan performed the same magnificent dunk, only this time he dribbled across the court before soaring for the climactic jam.

Twelve years later, Vince Carter permanently put his name in dunking lore when he stole the show during the 2000

At 5-7, Spud Webb shocked the basketball community when he won the 1986 Slam Dunk Contest in Dallas.

SKILLS CHALLENGE

Who is the best speed dribbler in the NBA? Who has the quickest crossover? Who is the most efficient performer when it comes to racing against the clock? The ultimate bragging-rights contest among NBA point guards, and an event that spotlights the skills necessary to fill one of the NBA's most demanding positions, the 989 Sports Skills Challenge made its debut during All-Star Saturday Night in 2003, and has become a staple in the NBA's weekend competition of skills events. It highlights the NBA's top point guards, as four players compete in a timed obstacle course consisting of dribbling, passing, and shooting stations.

Jason Kidd of the New Jersey Nets won the inaugural event in Atlanta, Georgia, in a contest against Gary Payton, Stephon Marbury, and Tony Parker.

Baron Davis of the New Orleans Hornets thrilled his hometown L.A. fans when he defeated Derek Fisher of the L.A. Lakers in the skills challenge at the Staples Center in 2004.

contest in Oakland, with his jaw-dropping between-the-legs, two-handed dunk.

"Improving the game is all about increasing the norm," said Jordan. "That's what we did in the slam dunk contest. Dr. J ran, I dribbled, and Vince Carter used two hands. That is the evolution of the dunk."

LONG-DISTANCE SPECIALISTS

A new event was added to the NBA All-Star Weekend in 1986, much to the delight of the NBA's premier shooters. The Long Distance Shootout made its debut in Dallas at Reunion Arena and featured Larry Bird, Sleepy Floyd, Dale Ellis, and Norm Nixon, among other great shooters. Players tested their long-range shooting skills from three different places beyond the three-point line in an attempt to convert as many field goals as possible within a one-minute time frame.

The event could have been renamed after the Celtics legend, Bird, who won the contest in its first three years. Specialized players such as Craig Hodges, Steve Kerr, and Tim Legler have gained newfound fame and notoriety after winning this event in later years.

Larry Bird of the Boston Celtics shoots a jump shot in the long-distance shooting contest during the 1988 All-Star Weekend in Chicago, Illinois.

All-Star Celebrations

WHILE THE WORLD'S GREATEST players converge on one city for a weekend of basketball skills, thrills, and all-around competition, other stars from the entertainment world also make the trip to be a part of the All-Star excitement. Whether it's to watch or participate in a celebrity-exhibition game, or to perform during half time of the All-Star Game, a wide range of talent—from actors to singers to comedians—makes the scene every year. Fans are also a huge part of the All-Star festivities, attending not only the games and contests but also the interactive Jam Session, visited by more than 300,000 people each year.

CELEBRITY GAME

Want to see your favorite hip-hop artist flawlessly perform a crossover dribble? Or your favorite actor drain a three? Celebrities from the entertainment industry aren't merely observers during the NBA's All-Star festivities—not when the league hosts its annual NBA Celebrity Game at Jam Session. Ashton Kutcher, P. Diddy, and Dean Cain are just some of the high-profile celebrities who have showcased their skills on center court over the years.

NBA JAM SESSION

A basketball fan's paradise, featuring more than 350,000 square feet of hoops fun, NBA Jam Session presented by Fleer offers a wide range of basketball activities for fans of all ages during the weeklong All-Star celebration. Whether it's launching a jump shot from a trampoline, shooting baskets with a slingshot, making a personalized trading card, or visiting with an NBA or WNBA player during an autograph session or basketball clinic, there certainly isn't a shortage of options. The Read to Achieve area features a reading zone where kids can hear celebrities and NBA or WNBA players share their favorite tale. Jam Session also features Club NBA, which showcases an array of chart-topping musical acts ranging from Nelly and Ja Rule to the Beach Boys.

Jason Kidd and Kenyon Martin of the New Jersey Nets arrive at the red carpet prior to the 2004 All-Star Game on February 15, 2004, at the Staples Center in Los Angeles, California.

A fan shoots the ball at the All-Star Jam Session in 2004. Jam Session is the world's largest interactive theme park.

READ TO ACHIEVE CELEBRATION

Every year, a star-studded lineup of music's biggest acts from music, television, and movies comes out in full force to celebrate the joys of reading and to highlight the NBA's Read to Achieve program by taking part in the league's Read to Achieve Celebration. Students from the All-Star host city attend as a reward for their participation in local reading programs.

Held on Saturday morning during All-Star Weekend and broadcast on more than 40 different networks, the event has featured the likes of recording superstars Christina Aguilera, Britney Spears, Justin Timberlake, LL Cool J, and Usher, as well as appearances by NBA and WNBA players who take an active part in the program throughout the season.

NBA PRESENTS BEYONCÉ

Singer Beyoncé Knowles performs during half time of the 2004 NBA All-Star Game on February 15, 2004, at the Staples Center in Los Angeles, California.

Yao Ming, Shaquille O'Neal, and headliner Christina Aguilera pose after the NBA All-Star Read to Achieve Celebration held at NBA Jam Session as part of the 2003 NBA All-Star Weekend.

ALL-STAR PERFORMANCES

The NBA All-Star Game is a global platform for top singers. Elton John, Mariah Carey, and Beyoncé Knowles are among the multi-platinum recording artists who have performed half-time shows for an audience of more than 800 million viewers around the world.

American and Canadian national anthems are also performed by top singers. Perhaps the two most memorable "Star-Spangled Banner" performances were Marvin Gaye's soulful rendition at the 1983 All-Star Game and his duet with his daughter, Nona, 21 years later at the 2004 All-Star Game.

Rock 'n' roll legend Elton John performs during half time of the 2002 NBA All-Star Game held in Philadelphia, Pennsylvania.

The WNBA Is Born

IN THE HISTORY OF WOMEN'S professional basketball, more than 15 leagues have failed, so why should the WNBA be any different? Visionary leadership, the backing of the 29 NBA teams, and the three-network partnership arrangement gave it an advantage unprecedented for a start-up sport. Once the TV partnerships were secured, players, teams, sponsorships, and merchandise soon followed. When the first game tipped off in 1997, more than 50 million viewers tuned in. Two years later, 37 broadcasters televised WNBA games to more than 125 countries in 17 languages. The league was unique, featuring an orange-and-oatmeal paneled ball and a catchy slogan: "We Got Next." And fans responded—more than a million walked through the arena turnstiles before the end of the first season.

WNBA PRESIDENT

As a former Academic All-American basketball player at the University of Virginia, Val Ackerman is passionate about the growth of women's sports and specifically the WNBA. Ackerman joined the NBA as a staff attorney in 1988, and headed a task force in 1993 to explore ways for the NBA to have an increased role in women's basketball, which resulted in the creation of the US Women's National Team that won the gold medal in the 1996 Olympics. Since her appointment as President of the WNBA in 1996, Ackerman has guided the league to new heights.

A LEAGUE OF THEIR OWN

The arrival of the WNBA in 1997 was the culmination of several trends—the surging popularity of women's college basketball both in attendance and ratings, the explosive growth of women's participation in sports in America, and the success of the gold-medal US Women's National Basketball Team in the 1996 Olympics.

The NBA's Board of Governors approved the concept of the WNBA on April 24, 1996, and by October the league had signed three former College Players

Sheryl Swoopes, Lisa Leslie, and Rebecca Lobo were the first three players to join the league in its infancy, providing a solid foundation.

of the Year: Sheryl Swoopes, Rebecca Lobo, and Lisa Leslie. Eight franchises soon followed: Charlotte, Cleveland, Houston, Los Angeles, New York, Phoenix, Sacramento, and Utah.

Unlike other women's leagues that had launched but ultimately failed due to a lack of exposure, a key component to the WNBA was its television coverage—33 games were broadcast on network and cable stations during its inaugural season. The league was also a hit at the gate as it averaged 9,669 fans during its three-month summer-season schedule. It was the most successful start-up of any professional sports league.

THE SMALL BALL

Introduced in 1997, the WNBA ball is one inch smaller in diameter than the men's ball, at 28.5 inches (72cm) in circumference, and weighs 2.5 ounces (70g) less. The first small ball actually made its debut prior to the 1984–85 season, and was immediately incorporated into girls' and women's leagues at all levels, with the exception of international play.

"The small ball came out my freshman year in college," said former WNBA All-Star center Vicky Bullett. "I liked it because it was lighter and I thought it made it easier for girls to shoot. I think it helps your range once you get used to playing with it."

The orange-and-oatmeal pattern gives the WNBA ball a distinctive look, as well as bringing another dimension to the game—viewing the rotation on a shot or a pass.

HISTORIC OPENING TIP

On June 21, 1997, less than 15 months after the NBA Board of Governors approved the concept of a Women's National Basketball Association, the dream became a reality when the Los Angeles Sparks hosted the New York Liberty for the league's inaugural game.

Before tip off, the Sparks lined up across a group of young fans and presented them with game balls. After tip off, the Sparks' Penny Toler etched her name in the record books by scoring the first two points in WNBA history. A raucous crowd of 14,284 filled the Great Western Forum, eager to cheer their heroines at every opportunity. "They even cheered for free throws," said 6-5 Sparks center Lisa Leslie.

"I've been waiting for this to happen and when it finally did, it was like an out-of-body experience," said 6-4 center Rebecca Lobo of the Liberty. "It felt great to finally be out here playing ball."

The Liberty defeated the Sparks 67-57.

WNBA President Val Ackerman tossed the ceremonial opening tip to mark the league's inaugural game on June 21, 1997, as Lisa Leslie of the Los Angeles Sparks (left) and Kym Hampton of the New York Liberty (right) eagerly anticipated the jump.

WNBA Milestones

ONE OF THE PRIMARY GOALS of the WNBA was to increase the exposure and popularity of women's basketball right from the start, and the league has met these objectives with great success. Over the league's first seven seasons, there have been a multitude of milestones, but some of the most memorable include the instant establishment of a Houston Comets dynasty and a single dynamic superstar, Cynthia Cooper, who would help increase the league's visibility during its infancy. Lisa Leslie's historic first dunk in women's professional basketball, Teresa Weatherspoon's miracle shot in the 1999 WNBA Finals, and the league's first foray overseas for an exhibition tour also top the list of great WNBA moments.

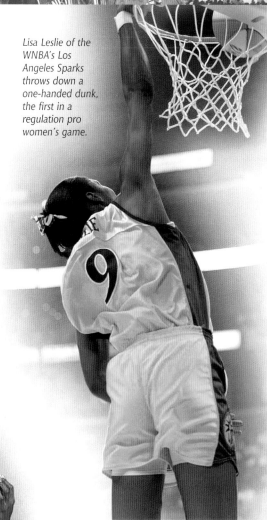

Lisa Leslie of the WNBA's Los Angeles Sparks throws down a one-handed dunk, the first in a regulation pro women's game.

The Houston Comets and coach Van Chancellor (second from right) claimed the WNBA's first four titles, from 1997–2000.

FIRST DYNASTY

With a nucleus of All-WNBA selections Cynthia Cooper, Sheryl Swoopes, and Tina Thompson, and the ever-consistent Janeth Arcain, the Houston Comets rolled to their first of four consecutive titles as the league's inaugural season concluded with a 65-51 victory over the New York Liberty on August 30, 1997.

But the most emotional championship of all was the team's third, captured in 1999. It was dedicated to Kim Perrot, the point guard from the team's first two titles who had worn jersey No. 10 and died of brain cancer a month prior to the 1999 WNBA Finals. As the seconds ticked down in the championship game, Cooper raised her hands, to give the referee's signal for No. 10. as the sellout crowd of 16,285 began chanting "three for Kim, three for Kim."

The Comets created Kim's Place, a facility for adolescent cancer patients at the University of Texas' M.D. Anderson Cancer Center.

MS. DUNK

On July 30, 2002, at the Staples Center in Los Angeles, L.A. Sparks center and founding WNBA player Lisa Leslie made history by becoming the first woman to dunk in a regulation professional game during the first half against the Miami Sol.

"I think it's awesome to see myself hanging up there on the rim," she said. "It was a cool moment in history that I obviously won't forget. . . . I was angry, actually. Our team, we weren't playing that well that night and we were down, losing. We got a legitimate steal, and I happened to just get out before everybody else, and I was angry, so I slammed it really hard."

"We were anticipating the moment and it was spectacular," Spark DeLisha Milton said.

Even some of Leslie's opponents, were pleased: "It was great for the women's game," the Sol's Debbie Black said.

Ms. MVP

Cynthia Cooper of the Houston Comets was the first player to be crowned the WNBA MVP after the league's inaugural season in 1997. Then, a year later, she became the first player to win the award twice. But most impressively, Cooper quickly approached permanent legend status by earning WNBA Finals MVP honors in each of the four Finals she and her teammates won between 1997–2000. All in all, Cooper completed a career that saw her play in five seasons, averaging 21.0 points and 4.9 rebounds.

A select team of WNBA All-Stars poses before the Cristo Redentor (Christ the Redeemer) statue on the Corcovado mountain in Rio de Janeiro, Brazil, during an international tour in September 1998.

THE SHOT

As the New York Liberty fought to stay alive in Game 2 of the best-of-three WNBA Finals on September 4, 1999, it seemed another sweep was on its way for the Houston Comets, who held a 67-65 lead. With under 2.4 seconds remaining, New York's Teresa Weatherspoon took the inbounds pass from teammate Kym Hampton, dribbled twice, and launched a desperate heave from behind the mid-court line. Somehow, it fell into the hoop, beating the buzzer as time expired, and putting the Comets' celebration on ice for one more day.

WNBA players stand before the Eiffel Tower in Paris, France, while on an international tour in 1997.

Teresa Weatherspoon on one of the most dramatic shots in the history of professional basketball: "When it left my hand it just looked like it was going in."

THE WNBA TOURS THE WORLD

In September 1998, a WNBA team featuring several of the league's leading players—including the Los Angeles Sparks' Lisa Leslie, the Washington Mystics' Nikki McCray, the New York Liberty's Rebecca Lobo, the Houston Comets' Cynthia Cooper, and the Orlando Miracle's Nykesha Sales—traveled to Brazil for several exhibition games and clinics. It was one of several trips the league has been involved in, as part of an effort to promote the women's game abroad.

WNBA team rosters are getting more international players than before as well—the 2003 season saw multiple players hailing from Australia, Brazil, Canada, the Czech Republic, and Russia, as well as 15 other countries.

The international players on this year's WNBA rosters include: the New York Liberty's Elena Baranova of Russia, the San Antonio Silver Stars' Margo Dydek of Poland, the Sacramento Monarchs' Ticha Penicheiro of Portugal, and the Seattle Storm's Lauren Jackson of Australia, 2003's WNBA MVP.

On May 6, 2004, the 2003 WNBA champions, the Detroit Shock, were joined by the San Antonio Silver Stars as the league's first teams to play outside the US, when they faced one another before a crowd of 13,536 in a preseason game in Monterrey, Mexico.

The WNBA Today

GREAT PLAYERS, GREAT MOVES, and great moments continue to be the theme in the WNBA. Players such as Chamique Holdsclaw, Tamika Catchings, and Sue Bird, all of whom enjoyed stellar collegiate careers, made instant impacts when they arrived in the WNBA. Off the court, the league continued to make a difference in the community with its involvement with the Read to Achieve and Breast Cancer Health Awareness programs. On the court, the Detroit Shock enjoyed a storybook finish by going from worst to first, winning the WNBA championship and, in the process, preventing the Los Angeles Sparks from achieving their three-peat.

As a rookie, Tamika Catchings finished second in scoring in the WNBA with 18.6 points per game.

In her WNBA debut, Sue Bird notched 18 points, six assists, three steals, and three rebounds against the New York Liberty.

SUE BIRD

Sue Bird's WNBA career immediately took flight. After guiding the University of Connecticut to two national titles in four years, the 2002 No. 1 overall draft pick rose quickly to the ranks of the WNBA elite. By the time she was 23, the Seattle Storm point guard earned two All-WNBA first-team selections in her first two years, and two starting berths on the Western Conference All-Star team. No one else has accumulated such accolades in her first two WNBA seasons.

CHAMIQUE HOLDSCLAW

After assembling one of the greatest college careers of all time—leading the University of Tennessee to three straight national titles—Chamique Holdsclaw continued her ascent with the WNBA's Washington Mystics, earning league Rookie of the Year honors in 1999, and performing breathtakingly ever since.

"What she means can't be measured. She has changed the face of women's sports," said track star Jackie Joyner-Kersee.

Chamique Holdsclaw led the league in both scoring and rebounding in her fourth season.

TAMIKA CATCHINGS

The anticipation for Tamika Catchings' debut in the WNBA was great. After sitting out the 2001 WNBA season while recovering from a torn right ligament, former University of Tennessee All-American Tamika Catchings made quite a splash in her rookie season with the Indiana Fever, earning WNBA Rookie of the Year honors after averaging 18.6 points and 8.6 rebounds and finishing third in the league's MVP voting. Catchings was also a force on the defensive end, finishing second in Defensive Player of the Year voting.

THE WNBA TODAY 149

DETROIT SHOCKS THE WNBA

The Detroit Shock made professional sports history when they defeated the Los Angeles Sparks for the 2003 WNBA Championship title. The Shock, which finished in last place in 2002, defeated the two-time defending WNBA champions with dramatic flair in the deciding Game 3 of the Finals series.

Ruth Riley of the Shock scored a career-high 27 points against one of the WNBA's premier players, Lisa Leslie, in front of the largest crowd in WNBA history, as 22,076 filled The Palace of Auburn Hills in Michigan.

The Shock became the first team in pro sports history to go from having the worst record in the league to become champions the next season.

Under former Detroit Pistons great Bill Laimbeer, the 2003 Detroit Shock made history by becoming the first team to go from last place to a championship within a single season.

THE WNBA AND READ TO ACHIEVE

Promoting the value of reading and online literacy, and encouraging families and adults to read regularly with young children, the WNBA's Read to Achieve Summer Reading Season tips off in May and includes many facets. All 13 WNBA teams conduct local Reading Time-Outs in their local market throughout the regular season, and work to establish a branded Reading Corner. The NBA/WNBA All-Star Reading teams are comprised of NBA and WNBA players and other members of the NBA/WNBA family—league officials, senior executives, as well as network broadcasters, hosts of NBA shows, celebrities, and government officials.

When Ruth Riley isn't scoring points on the court, she is scoring smiles with the kids of Read to Achieve.

BREAST HEALTH AWARENESS

In 2002, Edna Campbell (above, second from right) was the first active WNBA player to be diagnosed with breast cancer. A starter on the 2001 Sacramento Monarchs, Campbell, who missed most of the 2002 season to receive treatment, made a triumphant return to the Monarchs on August 13, 2002. The 5-8 guard played for 12 minutes during the Monarchs 59-51 victory. Since its inception in 1997, the WNBA and its teams have raised nearly $2,000,000 to aid in the fight against breast cancer.

The Naismith Memorial Basketball Hall of Fame

ALL SPORTS DESERVE A PROPER SALUTE and a nod to their glorious histories, and basketball isn't any different. The ultimate center of basketball greatness is located where basketball was born, in Springfield, Massachusetts, where for more than 35 years, the public has been welcomed to the Naismith Memorial Basketball Hall of Fame. As the game has grown to unparalleled heights of popularity, the need to remain modern, and to properly reflect the history and tradition of all levels of the game, has led to several relocations over the years. Despite the various facilities, one key component remains the same—it's still the place where every player wants to see his or her name.

It was a humble beginning for the Basketball Hall of Fame in 1968, when it resembled a traditional museum.

HALL(S) OF FAME

The first incarnation of the Naismith Memorial Basketball Hall of Fame opened in February 1968, in Springfield, Massachusetts, on the very campus where Dr. James Naismith first introduced the game some 77 years earlier, a site now belonging to Springfield College. For a period of time, the Hall of Fame had trophies and memorabilia, but no real theme. Nine years of inductions had gone on before it opened, so much of the focus was built around the early inductees.

As interest and funding increased, a new building was constructed across town along the Connecticut River, finally opening in 1985. This edition was conceived with chronological themes in mind and featured more sections.

As basketball mushroomed in popularity, steps were taken to create a state-of-the-art building that would be nearly double the size of its predecessor at 80,000 square feet. With a nine-story-high fiberglass sphere and a 15-story-high illuminated spire topped by a basketball, the new structure opened to great acclaim on September 29, 2002.

In 1985, the Hall of Fame moved across town to a 40,000-square-foot site along the Connecticut River.

On September 29, 2002, the Hall of Fame opened an entirely new, state-of-the-art facility that nearly doubled the size of the previous one, which stands nearby.

MEMORABILIA

When New Jersey Nets coach Lawrence Frank set a major league record with 13 consecutive victories at the start of his NBA coaching career on February 24, 2004, he found himself surprised to be asked to donate his necktie from that evening to the Hall of Fame. But once he knew where it was headed, he was more than happy to purchase another.

Throughout the Hall of Fame are rare photographs, historic game-worn uniforms, footwear, and other equipment. Some of the more notable pieces include: Wilt Chamberlain's 100-point-game jersey, All-Star Game jerseys belonging to Michael Jordan and Bill Russell, and shoes belonging to Bob Lanier (size 22) and Jordan (from his 1984–85 rookie season). Even arena fixtures, such as groups of seats from the original Boston Garden, Madison Square Garden, and Chicago Stadium abound in the Hall.

Game-worn uniforms, equipment, and footwear (shown in a glass case at right) are just some of the memorabilia visitors can enjoy at the new Hall of Fame. Also pictured are two interactive exhibits.

A fan compares his arm span to that of Chris Webber of the Sacramento Kings.

An interior shot of the globe at left shows the basketball court surrounded by the Honors Ring (above).

INTERACTIVE EXHIBITS

Among the attractions at the Hall of Fame are a state-of-the-art 200-seat theater, a high-school regulation–sized basketball court, and over a dozen interactive video kiosks that let visitors look up facts on their favorite teams, leagues, and players. Fans can participate in video games and trivia, skills competitions, and pick-up games. They can see how plays are broken down, call games like a broadcaster, or go head-to-head with a superstar via a virtual-reality computer. Visitors can even test their jumps against the pros'.

Hall of Fame Inductees

THE ORIGINAL CELTICS

In 1959, the Hall of Fame enshrined the first great professional team—the Original Celtics. Founded as the New York Celtics in 1914, the team re-formed as the Original Celtics under promoter James Furey in 1918, and dominated their competition on a barnstorming 200-game schedule, despite logging close to 150,000 miles of travel per season. The team included future Hall of Famers Nat Holman and Joe Lapchick, both of whom also became successful collegiate coaches.

THE ULTIMATE DESTINATION for any basketball player or fan is the Hall of Fame. The very foundation is built around the legends that have made the game what it is, whether they are male or female—collegians, professionals, or international inductees. Team inductees like the Original Celtics are joined by outstanding individual players, coaches, and contributors like Magic Johnson, Pat Summitt, and even a handful of multiple inductees, like John Wooden, Lenny Wilkens, and Bill Sharman. They are just a few of the 246 members of this immortal basketball family.

MAGIC JOHNSON

On September 27, 2002, Earvin "Magic" Johnson was officially enshrined into the Hall of Fame, but it was merely a formality as Johnson had already achieved basketball immortality many times over with one of the game's most memorable careers.

Only months after his Michigan State team defeated a Larry Bird–led Indiana State team in the 1979 NCAA championship game, Johnson and Bird made their respective ways into the NBA—Johnson with the L.A. Lakers and Bird with the Boston Celtics—where both led their teams to multiple championships and continued a rivalry so great that it was instrumental in the growth of fan enthusiasm for the NBA and led to a longtime friendship between the two legends. The respect between the two was evident at Johnson's enshrinement ceremony, where he was presented by none other than Larry Bird.

Magic Johnson speaks as he is inducted into the Basketball Hall of Fame at a ceremony held at the Springfield Civic Center on September 27, 2002.

Photos and information of all 246 (and counting) Hall of Fame inductees are on permanent display in the Honors Ring, the centerpiece of the basketball shrine.

Johnson concluded his playing career in 1996 as a five-time NBA champion, a three-time MVP of both the regular season and the Finals, a 12-time All-Star, and an Olympic gold medalist (1992).

Despite having been diagnosed with the virus that causes AIDS in 1991, he has shown no signs of slowing down his numerous business and community activities. A statue of him leading a fast break was unveiled outside the Los Angeles Staples Center in 2004.

Head coach Pat Summitt of the Tennessee Lady Vols speaks before presenting former head coach Leon Barmore of Louisiana Tech University at the Basketball Hall of Fame Enshrinement Ceremony on September 5, 2003.

PAT SUMMITT

The name Pat Head Summitt is synonymous with excellence in basketball. In 2000, the legendary University of Tennessee women's coach was inducted in the Hall of Fame, even though she's made it clear that she's nowhere near finished with her career.

In her 30-plus years of basketball, Summitt has amassed a record of 853-166 with the Lady Volunteers, and a winning percentage of .837, which is the best among coaches on both the women's and men's sides of the collegiate game. Only two other active coaches (Bob Knight of the Texas Tech men and Jody Conradt of the Texas Tech women) have surpassed the 800-win milestone.

Through the end of the 2003–04 season, Summitt is only 27 wins shy of becoming the winningest coach in the history of college basketball (both men's and women's programs), something she is on pace to accomplish within the next two seasons.

HONORS RING

Much of the design of the new Hall of Fame was centered around the belief that the enshrinees should be at the heart of the visitors' experience. Thus, the designers created the "Honors Ring," a ceremonial space suspended above the other galleries, dedicated to the people who have helped to make the game what it is.

As of mid-2004, a total of 246 individuals and five teams are saluted there. With enshrinees at the top of the ring, galleries below are arranged in a pyramid: The Game, The Players, The Media, The Coaches, and The Teams.

From players Kareem Abdul-Jabbar and George Yardley to coaches Forrest "Phog" Allen and Kay Yow, from contributors Senda Berenson Abbott and Fred Zollner to referees James Enright and David Walsh, all the Hall of Fame individuals are here, along with five team inductees: The First Team (inducted 1959), the Original Celtics (1959), the Buffalo Germans (1961), the New York Rens (1963), and the Harlem Globetrotters (2002).

PLAYER/COACH INDUCTEES

The Hall of Fame's most elite fraternity—those who have been enshrined as both a player and a coach—welcomed its third member in September 2004, as Bill Sharman joined John Wooden and Lenny Wilkens.

Sharman, inducted in 1976 as a player, is the only coach in history to win a title and be named Coach of the Year in three different leagues—the ABL's Cleveland Pipers (1962), the ABA's Los Angeles Stars (1970, co-Coach of the Year) and Utah Stars (1971, ABA

champions), and the NBA's L.A. Lakers (1972).

Wooden was enshrined as a player in 1961. As a coach (inducted in 1973), he was the architect of the greatest college dynasty in history: UCLA's ten NCAA championship teams, including seven in a row from 1966–73.

Wilkens was a nine-time NBA All-Star player from 1960–75, before going on to coach the Seattle SuperSonics (winning the 1979 NBA title), Portland Trail Blazers, Cleveland Cavaliers, Atlanta Hawks, Toronto Raptors, and his hometown New York Knicks in a 35-year career.

Lenny Wilkens

Bill Sharman

John Wooden

Index

Picture Credits

Ray Amati: 100 BR, 127 TL, 143 BL, 149 BL **Associated Press:** 10 TR, 35 CL, 90 BL **Bill Baptist:** 57 TC, 75 BL, 113 BL, 146 BL **Al Bello:** 79 BR **Andrew D. Bernstein:** 2-3, 12 BR, 14 BL, 15 T, 56 TL, 58 TR, 61 TL, 62-63, 68 BL, 74 TR, 74 BR, 77 BC, 79 BL, 79 C, 82-83, 95 BL, 99 BR, 103 TL, 107 BR, 111 TR, 113 BR, 116 LC, 116 TR, 127 R, 128 BR, 132 CR, 133 BL, 135 C, 139 TL, 140 BL, 141 TL, 141 TR, 145 BL, 153 BC, 135 BR **Lisa Blumenfeld:** 143 TR, 146 TR **Nathaniel S. Butler:** 5 BR, 15 CR, 67 T, 69 BL, 80 TR, 81 TR, 92 BCL, 130-131, 139 TR, 144 BL, 147 BL **Lou Capozzola:** 71 TR **Rich Clarkson:** 134 BR, 135 TR **Jim Cummins:** 54 R **Scott Cunningham:** 14 BC, 54 BCR, 55 TR, 70 B, 102 TL **Jonathan Daniel:** 56 BR, 64 R, 65 C, 67 BL, 72-73, 111 BL **Tim DeFrisco:** 101 TR, 105 R **Gary Dineen:** 102 BL, 142 BL **Stephen Dunn:** 70 TR, 97 R, 103 BR **Allen Einstein:** 76 TR **Garrett Ellwood:** 78 C, 111 BR, 118 BC, 140 TR **D. Clarke Evans:** 80 BR, 108 CL **Sam Forencich:** 99 TR, 106 BR **Steven Freeman:** 148 BC **Jesse D Garrabrant:** 80 BL, 81 BC, 89 T, 149 TL, 153 TL **Getty Images:** 66 BL, 66 R **Barry Gossage:** 125 TL, 126 TR **Noah Graham:** 114 TL, 124 BL **Otto Greule, Jr.:** 102 R, 153 BL **Andy Hayt:** 143 BR **Kent Horner:** 108 TR, 109 TR **Ron Hoskins:** 134 TR, 148 BR, 133 TL, 133 TR **Walter Iooss Jr.:** 11 R, 16-17, 41 BR, 45 TR, 46 R, 51 TC, 53 B, 65 TR, 91 BL, 141 BC **Walter Iooss Jr./Sports Illustrated:** 37 TL **Jed Jacobsohn:** 68 CL, 74 BL, 80 C, 95 TL, 100 BL, 139 BR **Glenn James:** 78 BL, 78 TR, 96 L, 125 TR,

126 C, 126 B **Ron Koch:** 50 TR **Vincent Laforet:** 75 TR **M. David Leeds:** 129 B **Neil Leifer:** 89 BL **Ken Levine:** 64 TL, 101 BR **Andy Lyons:** 94 R **Ronald Martinez:** 112 BR **Fernando Medina:** 75 BR, 77 R **Manny Milan/Sports Illustrated:** 61 BC **Zoran Milich:** 97 TL **Donald Miralle:** 76 BL **Joe Murphy:** 142 TR **Naismith Memorial Basketball Hall of Fame:** 4 BC, 4 TL, 5 TC, 8 TL, 8 BL, 8 C, 8 BR, 10 BR, 11 TL, 12 BC, 13 TL, 13 TR, 15 BR, 18 TR, 18 C, 18 BR, 19 TR, 19 CL, 19 BL, 20 TR, 20 C, 20 BL, 21 TL, 21 BL, 21 BR, 22 BL, 22 BC, 22 TR, 23 BL, 23 TC, 23 BR, 24 L, 24 C, 25 BC, 26 L, 26 R, 27 BL, 27 C, 27 CR, 27 BR, 29 TC, 30 TR, 30 BL, 30 C, 30 BR, 38 T, 38 C, 39 TR, 40 C, 40 TR, 41 TL, 41 BL, 41 TR, 44 R, 47 LT, 47 LB, 48 C, 49 TR, 50 BR, 54 BCL, 56 BL, 57 TL, 71 TL, 86 BL, 86 TR, 87 TL, 87 TR, 87 BL, 87 BR, 88 BL, 88 BC, 90 TR, 90 BR, 96 TR, 104 BL, 108 BR, 109 LC, 110 L, 110 TR, 110 BR, 113 TR, 138 R, 150 TL, 150 C, 150 BR, 151 TR, 151 BR, 152 TL, 152 TR **NBAE Photo Library:** 4 BL, 5 L, 8 TR, 9 BL, 9 CR, 9 BR, 9 TR, 10 BL, 11 BL, 12 BL, 12 TR, 13 BL, 13 CL, 13 CR, 14 TR, 15 BL, 24 R, 25 L, 25 RT, 25 RC, 25 RB, 27 TL, 27 TC, 27 TR, 28 R, 29 BL, 29 TR, 29 RT, 29 RC, 29 RB, 31 TL, 31 TC, 31 CB, 31 CR, 31 BR, 32 L, 34 TL, 34 BL, 35 TL, 35 TC, 35 TR, 35 CCT, 35 CCB, 37 RT, 37 RCT, 37 RCB, 37 RB, 38 BL, 38 BR, 39 BL, 40 BL, 44 L, 45 LT, 45 LC, 45 LB, 45 BC, 46 BL, 47 LCT, 47 LC, 47 LCB, 48 TR, 49 TC, 49 BR, 50 L, 51 TR, 51 BL, 51 BC, 51 BR, 54 BL, 55 BCL, 55 BCR, 55 BL, 55 BR, 57 C, 57 BLT, 57 BL, 57 BR, 59 BL, 59 BR, 60 BL, 60 BC, 61 TR, 64

BL, 65 BL, 65 BC, 65 BR, 67 BCR, 67 BR, 69 TL, 69 TR, 71 BL, 71 BR, 78 TL, 91 BR, 92 TL, 92 TC, 92 TR, 92 BL, 92 BCR, 93 TC, 93 TR, 93 CT, 93 CC, 93 BL, 93 BCL, 93 BC, 93 BCR, 93 BR, 95 TR, 98 TL, 98 BL, 104 TR, 105 L, 109 BC, 114 B, 115 CL, 115 BR, 116 BR, 117 TC, 117 TCR, 117 TR, 117 LCT, 117 LC, 117 BL, 117 BCL, 117 BCR, 117 BR, 118 TL, 119 BC, 120 TR, 120 BL, 120 BCL, 120 BCR, 120 BR, 121 TL, 121 TR, 121 BR, 122 TL, 122 TR, 122 LC, 122 BL, 122 BR, 123 TL, 123 TC, 123 TR, 123 CT, 123 CL, 123 CR, 123 B, 132 TR, 132 BL, 134 BL, 138 TL, 138 BC, 144 TR, 145 TR, 147 TL, 147 BR, 153 BR **Juan Ocampo:** 142 BR **Doug Pensinger:** 103 BL **Norm Perdue:** 14 BR, 68 R **Hy Peskin/Sports Illustrated:** 84-85 **Portland Trail Blazers:** 6-7 C **Jennifer Pottheiser:** 129 TR, 147 TR, 151 CR, 152 BR **Mike Powell:** 60 TR **Dick Raphael:** 35 BR, 36 R, 42-43 C, 47 TR, 48 BL, 90 RC, 94 L, 112 TR, 58 BL, 59 L, 59 TR **Ken Regan:** 34 TR, 36 BL, 37 BL **Jeff Reinking:** 81 LC, 127 BL **Wen Roberts:** 105 C **Ezra Shaw:** 98-99 C, 125 BL **David Sherman:** 69 BR, 88 R, 124 TL **Tom Smart:** 64 BC **Kent Smith:** 77 BL, 100 TR **Catherine Steenkeste:** 92 BR, 115 BL, 118 BR, 128 TR **Rick Stewart:** 91 TR, 101 L **Noah Trotman:** 125 BR **Noren Trotman:** 13 BR, 104 CR **Ron Turenne:** 97 BL **Turner Sports:** 119 TL **Turner Sports; ABC/ESPN:** 118 BL **Terrence Vaccaro:** 114 TR **Jerry Wachter:** 49 L, 89 BR **Rocky Widner:** 103 TR, 119 TR, 128 LC, 148 TL, 149 BR

Acknowledgments

This ultimate book on basketball was assembled by a flawless team of ultimate professionals whose commitment to excellence was second to none. The NBA would like to especially thank Anja Schmidt, Dirk Kaufman, Susan St. Louis, Tai Blanche, Chrissy McIntyre, Milos Orlovic, Chris Avgherinos, Sharon Lucas, and Tina Vaughan at DK.

Thank you to Charlie Rosenzweig, Joe Amati, Michael Levine, Scott Yurdin, Brian Choi, and Todd Caso. And a special thank you to Matthew Krautheim and John Fawaz who assisted as the shot clock was set to expire.

Last but not least, thanks to the ultimate Hall of Famer and person, Bill Walton, whose contributions made this project complete.

DK would like to thank Claire Legemah and Nick Harris for their hard work on getting this book out on schedule, John Searcy for his excellent proofreading ability and all his other help, Jennifer Williams for some last-minute assistance, Nanette Cardon and IRIS for their usual superb index, and Joshephine and Katherine Yam and the team at Colourscan.